Gerhard Richter

STRIP-TOWER

F L I P B O O K

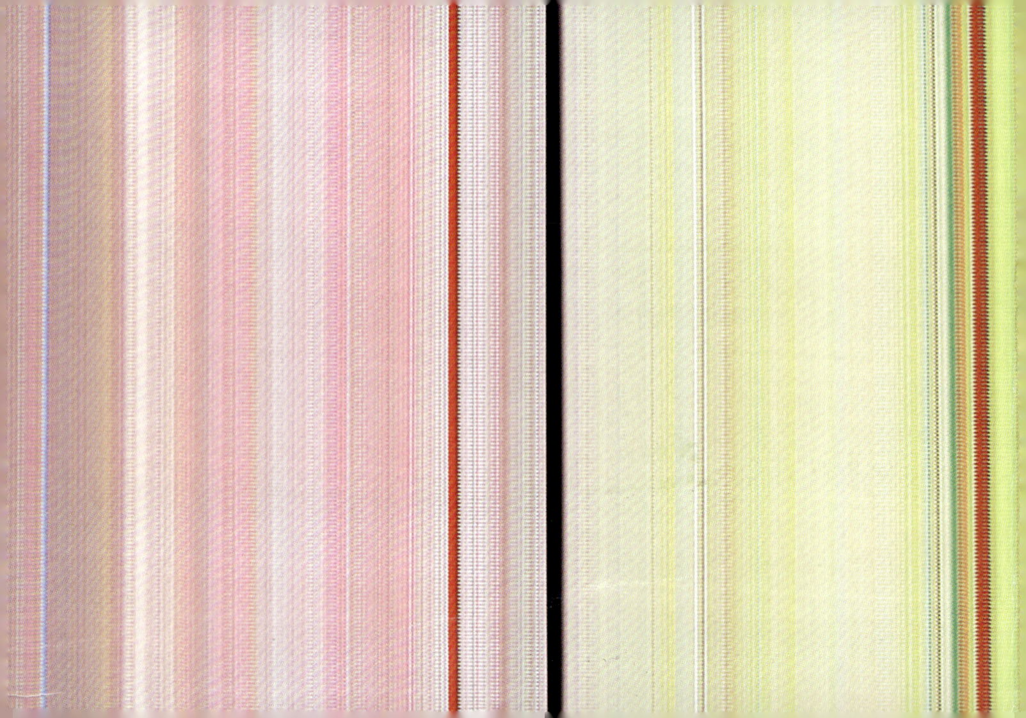

PREFACE

Since the early 1960s, Gerhard Richter (b. 1932, Dresden, Germany; lives and works in Cologne, Germany) has tirelessly explored the infinite possibilities of painting and become a celebrated artist worldwide. *STRIP-TOWER* (962), 2023 – a new public sculpture presented at Serpentine in Kensington Gardens between April 2024 and February 2025 – expanded on the artist's enduring investigations of painting, photography, digital reproduction and abstraction. Building on his series of *Abstraktes Bild* (*Abstract Painting*), which are composed through a unique technique of dragging paint across the surface of the canvas to create a textured field of colour, this approach was translated into three dimensions for presentation in the public realm. The sculpture was produced in close collaboration with Joe Hage, founder of HENI, whose team undertook many experiments to identify the technology for printing onto a ceramic surface.

Since 2011, Richter has developed a series of *Strip Paintings* created by photographing and digitally manipulating a painting, laminating the image onto aluminium and covering it with Perspex. These were inspired by an earlier 'squeegee painting' titled *Abstract Painting* (724-4), 1990, which was photographed and, with the support of computer software, the scanned images were digitally manipulated and divided into two strips, then four, eight, sixteen and thirty-two. The vertical strips of the painting were then stretched across a horizontal expanse before being laminated onto aluminium and covered with Perspex.

STRIP-TOWER (962) employs a similar method, in which colourful striped ceramic tiles clad two perpendicular panels. The thin vertical stripes form a dense and colourful composition, where the intersecting panels create a cross section within which visitors could stand. Building on the artist's ongoing interest in the concept of reflection, both materially and conceptually, the reflective surfaces of the glossy tiles subtly mirrored the viewer and the surroundings of Kensington Gardens. Like his *Strip Paintings*, *STRIP-TOWER* (962) fractures the picture plane and outside world.

With *STRIP-TOWER* (962), Richter revisits his concerns with reflections, systems and repetitions, previously seen in *4900 Colours* (901), a kaleidoscopic work comprising 196 square panels of 25 coloured squares each that were conceived to be configured in a number of variations. This was presented at Richter's acclaimed solo exhibition at Serpentine South in 2008 and in the accompanying catalogue. *4900 Colours* in part grew out of Richter's design for the south transept window of Cologne Cathedral, which replaced the plain glass window that was installed after the original stained glass had been destroyed during the Second World War. Richter's window, unveiled in August 2007, features 11,500 hand-blown squares of glass in 72 colours derived from the palette of the original medieval glazing. An arbitrary distribution of colours was generated using a specially developed computer programme, and this interest in using chance composition is discussed in depth in Professor Marcus du Sautoy's essay for this book, which also applies mathematics to establish whether there is an optimal viewing position from which to look at *STRIP-TOWER* (962).

We are honoured that Gerhard Richter accepted our invitation to present this work at Serpentine. It has been a great privilege to work with him again and we are enormously grateful for the continued energy and dedication he has given to this project. Our appreciation is also extended to Sabine Moritz, who has been supportive of this project from the beginning and engaged in many useful dialogues throughout.

Staging a project of this ambition would not be possible without the commitment of many individuals and organisations. We would like to express our gratitude to HENI, in particular Joe Hage. His ongoing support and collaboration with Serpentine were crucial in bringing this public sculpture to life. Joe also conceived the concept of photographing the sculpture in the round at five-degree intervals and presenting the images in book form to echo the experience of walking around the artwork. Additional thanks go to Bruce Cameron, who worked closely on the construction, and Hinnerk Meyer at Grieger GmbH. We would also like to thank AECOM, DP9, Gallowglass Health and Safety, and Mtec Fine Art, who provided essential expertise to help fulfil the ambitions of our public art projects. Our deepest thanks go to the Royal Parks team, our long-term collaborators, for supporting our vision in bringing Richter's work to Kensington Gardens. We especially thank Andrew Williams, Park Manager, for his guidance and support. Our gratitude extends to Google Arts and Culture for their generous support and collaboration.

Photography for this book is by Antony Mackinson of Prudence Cuming Associates Ltd, and we would also like to express our thanks to the HENI Publishing team for proposing and creating the publication in two formats: a conventional catalogue and this flipbook. The book was designed by Sylvia Ugga, working with colleagues Rod Hare, Director; Rebecca Morrill, Executive Commissioning Editor; and Sarah McLaughlin, Production and Publications Manager.

We are grateful to the eminent mathematician Marcus du Sautoy, Simonyi Professor for the Public Understanding of Science at the University of Oxford; Fellow of New College, Oxford; and author of numerous bestselling mathematics and science books for his essay. Marcus first encountered Richter's work when he delivered a public talk at the Serpentine during Richter's exhibition

4900 Colours in 2008 and returned repeatedly to participate in the Serpentine's annual *Marathon* series, continuing to marry art with mathematical principles in ways that are both compelling and engaging. We are delighted to include his perspective on Richter's sculpture in this book.

We would like to offer our continued thanks to Bloomberg Philanthropies, in particular to our Chairman Michael R. Bloomberg, Patti Harris and Jemma Read, for partnering with us on Serpentine's Bloomberg Connects App, which enables us to extend the reach of our audiences. The Serpentine International Council is an extraordinary group of individuals who provide ongoing and important assistance, in enabling us to deliver our ambitious Art, Architecture, Civic, Ecologies, Education, Live and Technology Programmes. We are also sincerely appreciative of the support from the Corporate Members, Americas Foundation, Patrons and Future Contemporaries of Serpentine. The public funding that Serpentine receives through Arts Council England provides an essential contribution towards all of our work and we remain grateful for their continued commitment.

Finally, we would like to express our deep appreciation to the Serpentine team whose hard work and dedication have made this project possible: Julie Burnell, Director of Construction and Special Projects; Lizzie Carey-Thomas, Interim Director of Programmes and Chief Curator; Chris Bayley, Exhibitions Curator; and our beloved Mike Gaughan, Gallery Manager. They worked closely with the wider Serpentine staff to bring this project to fruition.

Hans Ulrich Obrist, Artistic Director
Bettina Korek, Chief Executive

DECODING RICHTER'S STRIP-TOWER

Marcus du Sautoy

In *STRIP-TOWER* (962), 2023, Gerhard Richter achieves the extraordinary act of capturing complexity and simplicity in one striking sculpture. The complexity is embodied in the intricate variety of colour changes that occur as your eyes scan horizontally across the surface. And yet, move in a perpendicular direction and simplicity holds court. Every vertical line is a single colour that sweeps from bottom to top of the sculpture. But how is this image achieved? What decisions were made to determine the overall choice of colours?

The process actually begins with an image that has complexity in both dimensions. The origin of the *STRIP-TOWER* (962) is one of Richter's earlier paintings, *Abstract Painting* (724-4), 1990, which layers, smudges and erases paint in a process that results in a canvas of huge, almost fractal complexity. Richter then came up with an ingenious way to 'see' that complexity, resulting in the strip images that are used in the tower.

The process starts by dividing the painting vertically into two halves, which are then mirrored to create two new paintings. The symmetry in each image contrasts with the highly random and chaotic nature of the paint on the canvas. Richter had already played a similar game with the huge stained-glass window that he was commissioned to create for Cologne Cathedral (900), 2007, which takes its inspiration from his work *4096 Colours* (359), 1974 – one of a number of colour chart paintings the artist produced that used chance as a means of randomly arranging the colours. The window was produced in parallel with the multi-part painting, *4900 Colours* (901), 2007. It comprises 196 panels, each one a five-by-five grid of squares, where the colours of the squares are chosen at random from a selection of 25 different possible colours. The same idea of random choices of colours was used to create the stained-glass window, but in the cathedral, there is an extra element of symmetry: Richter mirrors the random choice. The left-hand side of the window consists of an array of square pieces of glass whose colours are all chosen randomly. But the right-hand side is a reflection of the left, making something rather like a stained-glass Rorschach inkblot.

The reason that the Swiss psychoanalyst Hermann Rorschach chose to make inkblots with symmetry is that the human brain is incredibly sensitive to images with symmetry. In the chaos of the jungle, an image with left-right symmetry is likely to be an animal, which could either eat you or you could eat it. Either way, the brain that recognises symmetry is the brain that survives. This is why the human species has evolved to be hypersensitive to symmetry. Symmetry conveys a message that helps us to survive and navigate our environment. But what Rorschach recognised is that we are so attuned to reading messages in symmetrical forms that we will imbue any symmetrical image with meaning, and the story we tell will often be a window into our own inner world.

And it is certainly the case that there seems to be more of a story embedded in the images that Richter makes with that first division of the abstract painting into two symmetrical paintings. But then Richter decided to repeat the process again. This time, the image was divided into four vertical strips. Each one was taken individually and repeated four times across the canvas, reflecting the image each time as you went. The effect is to create a symmetrical image repeated twice. It's symmetry within symmetry.

Having started the algorithm going, it is clear where Richter would take it next. Divide the painting into eight vertical strips. And now use each strip to create a new canvas where the strip is repeated eight times, again reflected each time it is laid down. The process has generated eight new images that are a mix of symmetry and chaos.

The striking thing is that once you push this algorithm to its limit, dividing the image by two each time, there comes a point where the horizontal chaos disappears. Instead, by the time you've halved the image twelve times, creating 4,096 different vertical strips, and then taken each of these strips individually and repeated it across the composition, reflecting the piece each time, you are left with an image that is a sequence of horizontal coloured lines. A vertical strip that is 1/4096th of the whole canvas reaches a point where the horizontal structure at any point appears to be a single colour. The repetition across the canvas then simply copies this colour horizontally across the canvas to create the coloured lines.

It is striking to ask at what point is structure lost and these lines emerge? If you follow the process that Richter applies to his abstract painting, it takes halving the canvas twelve times for this to happen. Contrast this, for example, if he'd started with one of his panels from *4900 Colours* (901). This consists of a five-by-five array of randomly coloured squares. After just halving it three times so that your vertical strip represents 1/8th of the panel, then four out of the eight vertical strips will not change with further division. You have already reached the limit of the complexity. But there is something interesting that happens because five is an odd number. There will be a vertical strip that always retains the two colours of the adjacent squares. What this process is doing is picking up regions of stability but also moments of phase change. It is also a measure of how far one needs to zoom in before a fractal quality to an image vanishes.

The vertical complexity of the original image is now captured in the intricate variety of colour that one sees as one scans down the lines. The 'decision' about these colours was made at the point that Richter worked adding layer upon layer to his abstract painting, pushing and pulling the paint across the canvas. With Richter's five-by-five array of colours, you will only ever get five horizontal lines of colour. But if you take another image, such as Leonardo da Vinci's *Mona Lisa,* then this process produces a much more gradual transition of colour from top to bottom reflecting the reduced complexity of the image compared to Richter's *Abstract Painting* (724-4). Richter's process applied to the *Mona Lisa* results in large bands of horizontal colour that correspond to the skin of the face or the green of the sky or the brown of the clothes.

In the case of *Abstract Painting* (724-4), where has the horizontal complexity gone? At the final stage of the process there are 4,096 canvases. Each canvas is made from the reflection and repetition of a strip representing 1/4096th of the whole canvas. The complexity of the horizontal dimension is now embodied in the fact that these 4,096 canvases are all so different. If you go from the canvas made from strip number 2367 to the next canvas made from strip number 2368, they look completely different.

If one takes one of the panels of *4900 Colours* (901) and considers the strip one gets from, for example, the transition from red to green, then this strip gets thinner and thinner while still retaining the switch from red to green. So Richter's process creates ever thinner strips that alternate between red and green. At first, the eye can easily see these transitions. But at some point the physiology of the eye means that we can no longer make the distinction. The cones in our eye receive data of a mix of red and green. The brain then interprets this as a single colour: yellow. In some sense, this is what is happening regardless of the section we start with. There will be regions where the colour of the paint changes from one to the other. One choice of strip will always retain this moment of transition (unless it happens to occur at exactly a point that is a power of 1/2). So the repeated halving and repetition will produce a single colour at the point where the change from one colour to the next is so small that the eye can't resolve it. As Richter has discovered, this seems to happen when the strip is 1⁄4096th of the whole canvas. The canvas of *Abstract Painting* (724-4) is 126 cm in width. So we are getting down to a strip that is 0.3 mm wide.

This property is at the heart of how a TV produces colours from combinations of red, green and blue pixels. An Ultra HD display consists of exactly 3840 × 2160 pixels, which amounts to 8,294,400. Each pixel has a size of 0.375 mm. Each pixel is divided into three subpixels of 0.125 mm width, representing the primary colours red, green and blue. These are sufficiently small for combinations set at different intensities to produce any colour the eye can perceive. So alternating red-green subpixels will produce a yellow colour across the screen. Richter's 'subpixels' are 0.3 mm across, which is sufficiently small to trick the eye in a similar way. This is equivalent to a Full HD (1080p) TV, which has a resolution of 1920 × 1080, resulting in 2,073,600 pixels with a pixel size of 0.635 mm.

The original *Strip Paintings* that Richter created consist of horizontal strips. But for *STRIP-TOWER* (962), Richter has chosen to divide the image horizontally rather than vertically, creating vertical lines of colour. This has an interesting impact on the sculpture. One of the challenges of the piece is that it is impossible to see the whole sculpture because it is no longer just a two-dimensional canvas but a three-dimensional structure. It therefore invites you, the viewer, to move in space to understand the piece in its entirety. But is there an optimal point from which to view the piece in order to take in as much of the surface as possible? This is a challenge that any photographer capturing a single still image of the piece faces.

If you look at the photos that have been taken, you can see that the photographer often choses to frame the surface of one complete quadrant while including something of the adjacent quadrant. Had Richter chosen horizontal lines of colour, this would have had an impact on the information that the photo would capture. Because we know that the colours on the adjacent, partially covered surface continue horizontally, we would not essentially lose any information from this partial view. But by choosing vertical strips of colour instead, this is not the case. We have no clue as to the colours that are hidden from view because the visible portion holds no information about how the image continues. Therefore, it becomes a challenge to choose a point that offers as much of the adjacent wall as is possible.

Mathematically, if we position ourselves such that the angle to the acute wall is infinitesimally small and we position ourselves at an infinite distance from the sculpture, then this position maximises the area in view (essentially three full sides minus an infinitesimally small strip). However, there is clearly a problem with this. We are physical embodied beings with visual limitations and don't live in an idealised mathematical realm. Although an angle of epsilon will mean that formally we can see the whole side of the wall, in reality it will be a blur. Our physiology can't decode the visual information that this small slither is revealing to us.

Each of us will need to establish an angle, with the wall that juts towards us providing a sense that we can 'see' the detail. Similarly, each of us will have a distance from the sculpture that allows us to 'see' the detail of the other walls. Too near and we are obscuring too much of the adjacent wall. Too far and we lose information about the detail of the changing colours. For example, if the distance between colour changes makes an angle of less than 1/60th of one degree from our position then it is generally accepted that a person with average vision can't pick out this level of detail. This means that the sculpture engages with our senses in an embodied and personal manner, depending on each individual's physiology.

Mathematics of how to view the *STRIP-TOWER*

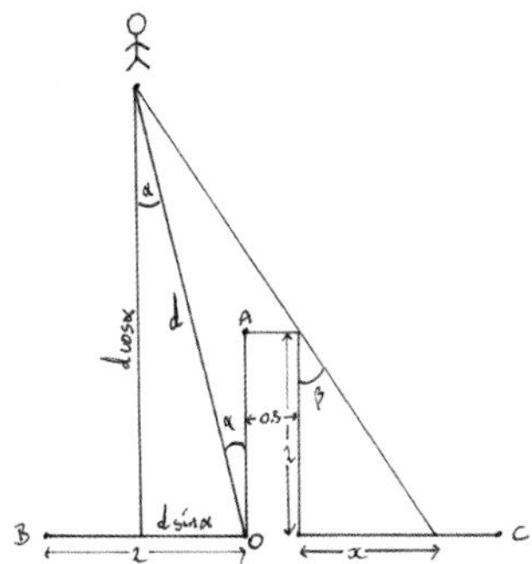

You want to position yourself so that you see as much of the far wall as possible, but to do this you will sacrifice the detail that you can see on the acute wall AO.

Let x denote the length of the far wall that you cannot see $0 \le x \le 2$.

For any given choice of distance, there is going to be an optimal position along the line extended from the far wall to the corner, which will minimise the length over which you lose the ability to see detail. For a person with average vision, this is 1/60 of a degree or $1/(360 \times 60)$ of the circumference of the circle. If is the distance from the viewer to the point O where the two walls meet, then this distance is $2\pi d/(360 \times 60)$.

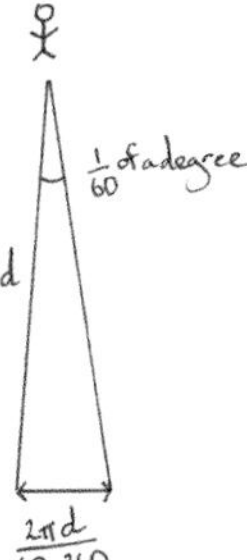

But because the wall is at an angle α, the length along the wall AO that we can no longer distinguish detail is:

$r = 2\pi d/(360 \times 60 \times \sin\alpha)$.

Let's set $k = (360 \times 60)/2\pi$ to simplify our formulas.

So the point is to choose the angle α to minimise this. We will need to know d in terms of α and x. Comparing similar triangles we get:

$(d \sin\alpha + 0.5 + x)/(d \cos\alpha) = \tan\beta = x/2$

Solving for d we get:

$d = (1 + 2x)/(x \cos\alpha - 2 \sin\alpha)$

So the resolution is:

$r = (1 + 2x)/(k \sin\alpha\, (x \cos\alpha - 2 \sin\alpha))$

Remember that we have fixed x so we want to minimise this, which means maximising the inverse

$k \sin\alpha\, (x \cos\alpha - 2 \sin\alpha)/(1 + 2x)$

With x fixed, we differentiate with respect to α:

$(kx (\cos\alpha)^2 - 4k \cos\alpha \sin\alpha - kx (\sin\alpha)^2)/(1 + 2x)$

So we are interested in the point where this is 0, which gives us the angle that will minimise r.

For example, here is the graph for $x = 1$ (which represents seeing half of the far wall).

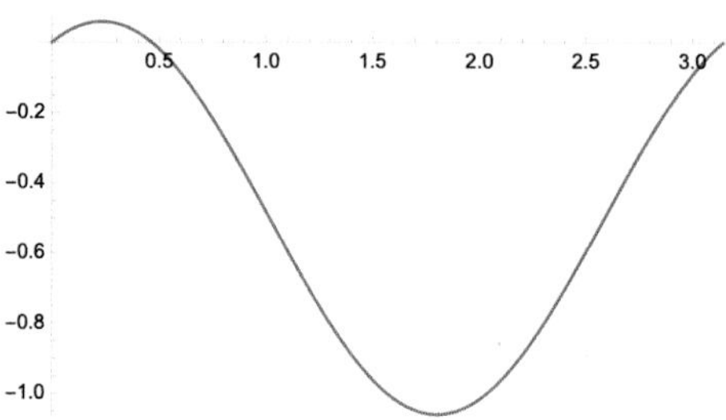

The value of the maximum is at $\alpha = 0.231824$ (in radians), which is 13.28 degrees. This is a distance of 5.83949 metres from O, the point where the walls meet. The resolution distance is then 7.39 mm.

Here is a table for various different values of x:

x	α (in radians)	r (in m)	d (in m)	α (in degrees)
0.5	0.122489	0.0189033	7.94006	7.018108665
1	0.231824	0.00739333	5.83949	13.28254801
1.5	0.321751	0.00465421	5.05964	18.43498993
1.75	0.359415	0.00398152	5.05964	20.59297999
2	0.392699	0.00351133	4.6194	22.50001432

Alternatively, you might want to start by deciding the level of detail that you want to have in view on the acute wall AO. If you are at an angle of α to the acute wall and a distance of d from the intersection O then recall that the length where detail blurs is $r = 2\pi d/(360 \times 60 \times \sin\alpha)$

At this position we have x of the far wall obscured. Having fixed r we want to choose (d, α) to minimize x.

Recall that we set $k = (360 \times 60)/2\pi$ to simplify our formulas. Then we can write $d = k \times r \times \sin\alpha$

What is the value of x? Recall above that we used similar triangles to write x in terms of (d, α): $(d\sin\alpha + 0.5 + x)/(d\cos\alpha) = \tan\beta = x/2$

Substituting the expression for d gives: $x = (2kr(\sin\alpha)^2 + 1)/(kr(\sin\alpha\cos\alpha) - 2)$

We need to find the value of alpha that minimises this. Here we apply some calculus: $dx/da = (4kr(\sin\alpha\cos\alpha))/(kr(\sin\alpha\cos\alpha) - 2) + (kr(\cos\alpha)^2 - kr(\sin\alpha)^2)(2kr(\sin\alpha)^2 + 1)/(kr(\sin\alpha\cos\alpha) - 2)^2$

For a given choice of resolution r we then find the value of α that makes $dx/da = 0$. This is the point that minimises x. So, for example, choosing $r = 0.005$ m = 5 mm then $\alpha = 0.305775$ radians = 17.52 degrees, which gives $d = 5.17436$ m, which obscures $x = 1.40246$ m of the far wall. This fits with the calculations we did starting from fixing x.

Views from the
Serpentine Gallery 2024

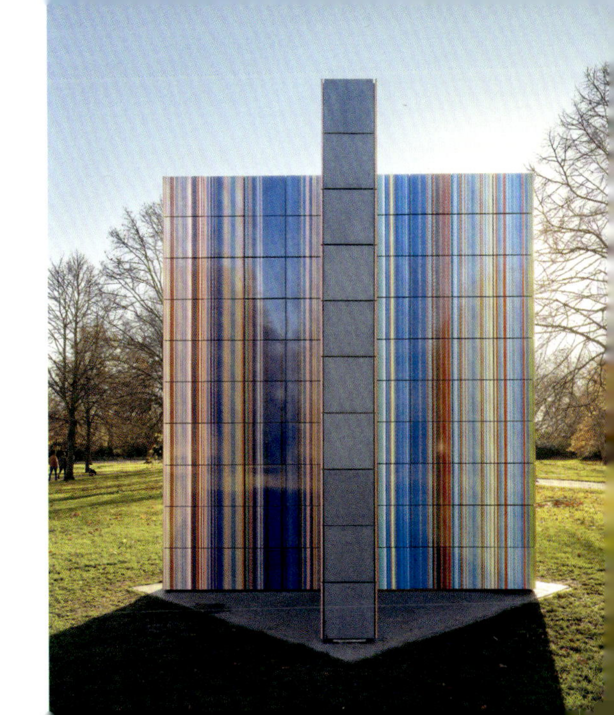

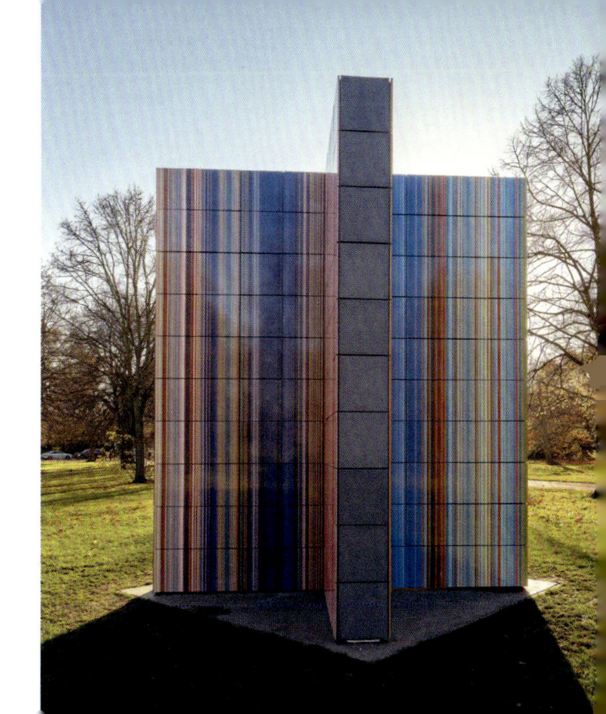

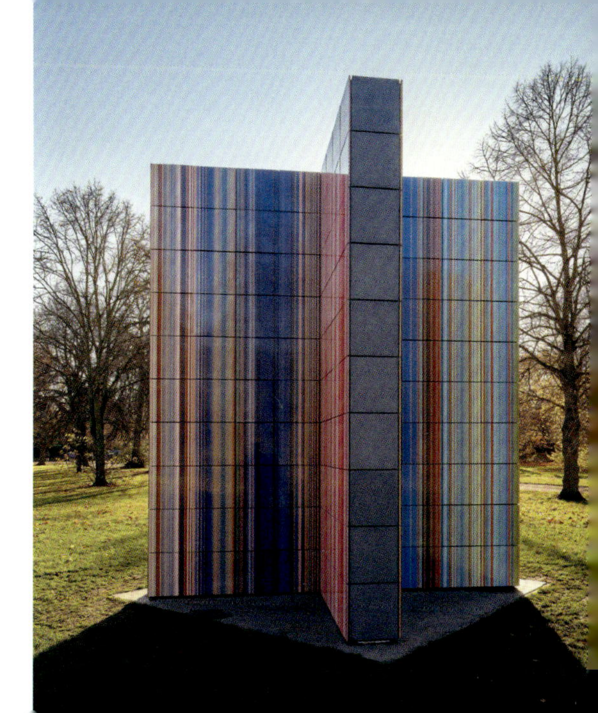

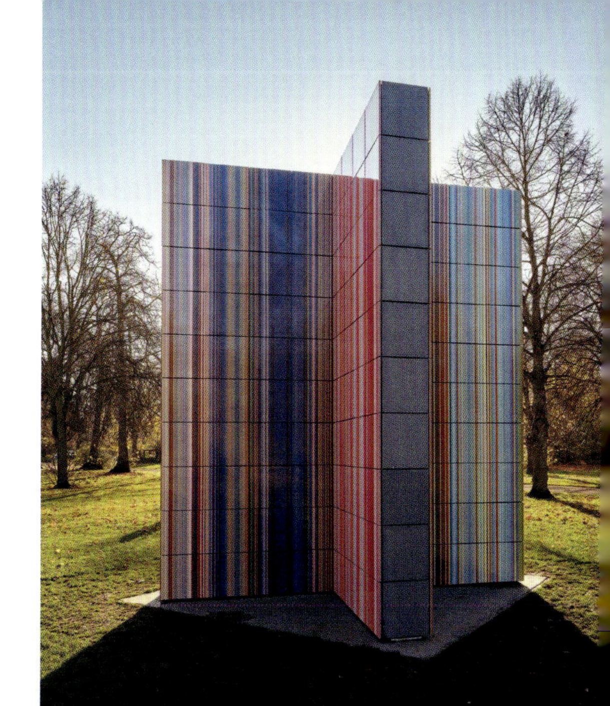

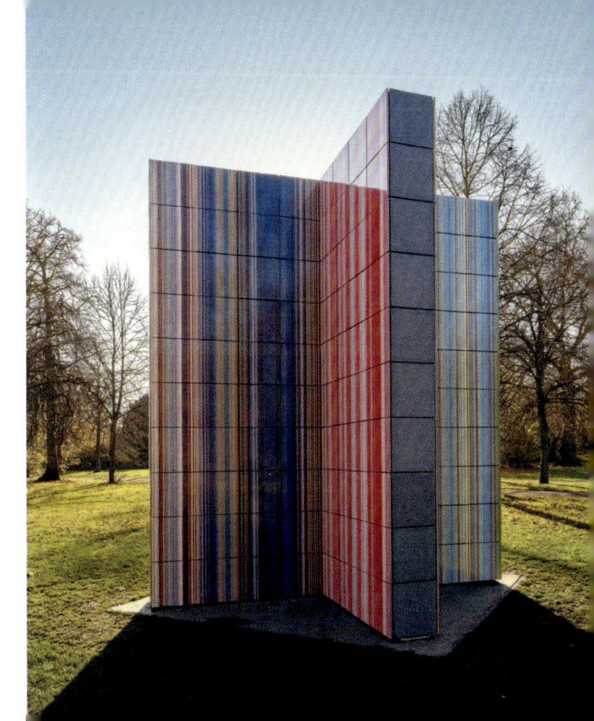

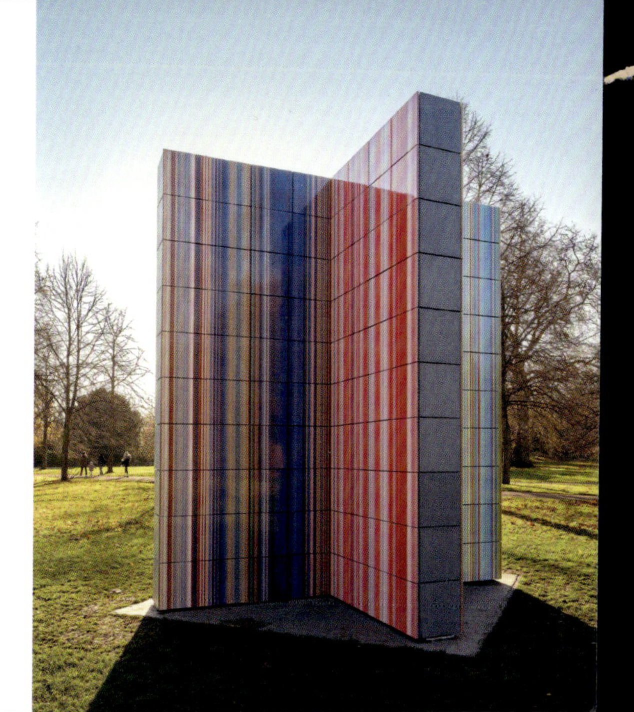

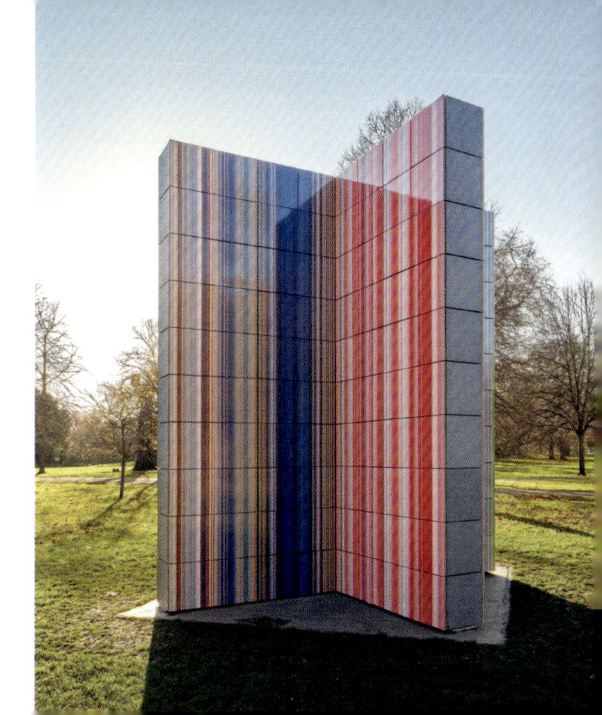

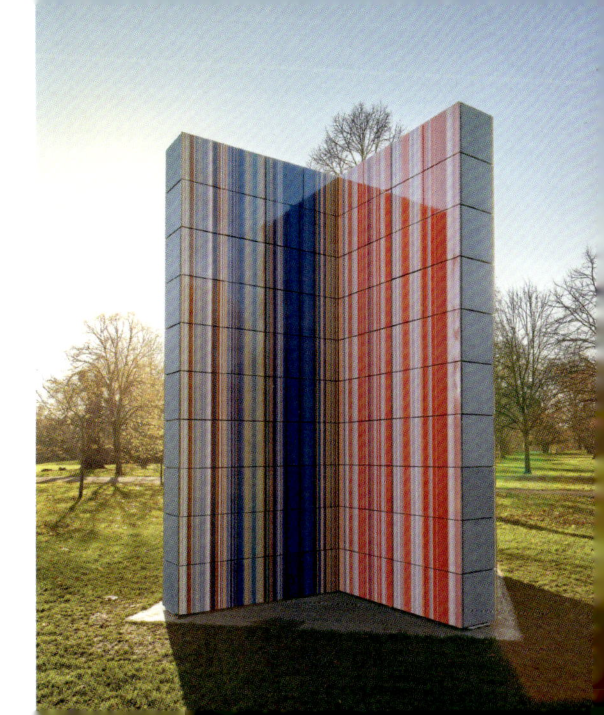

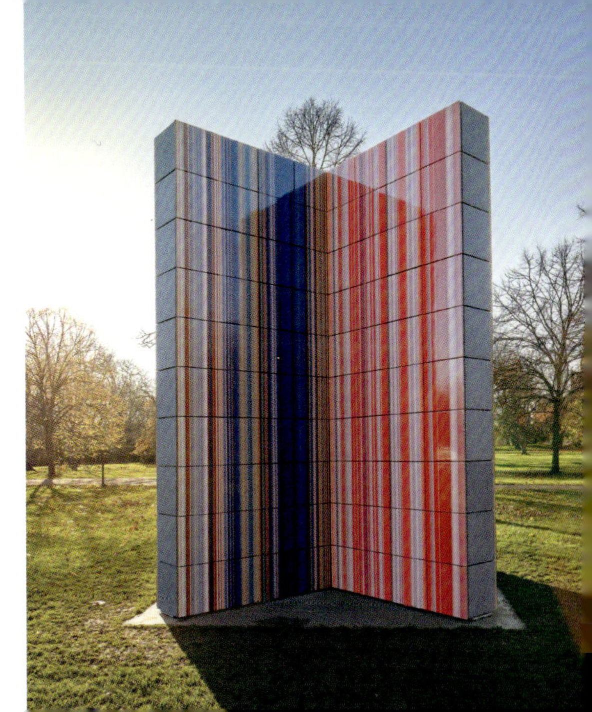

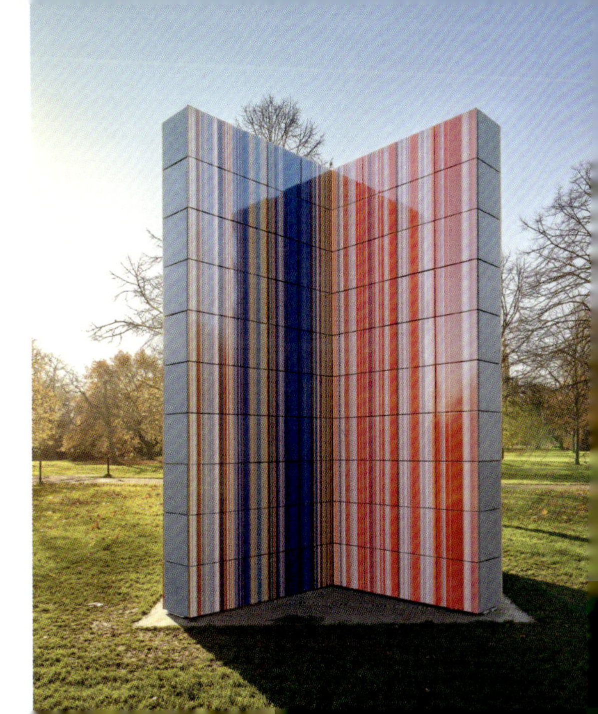

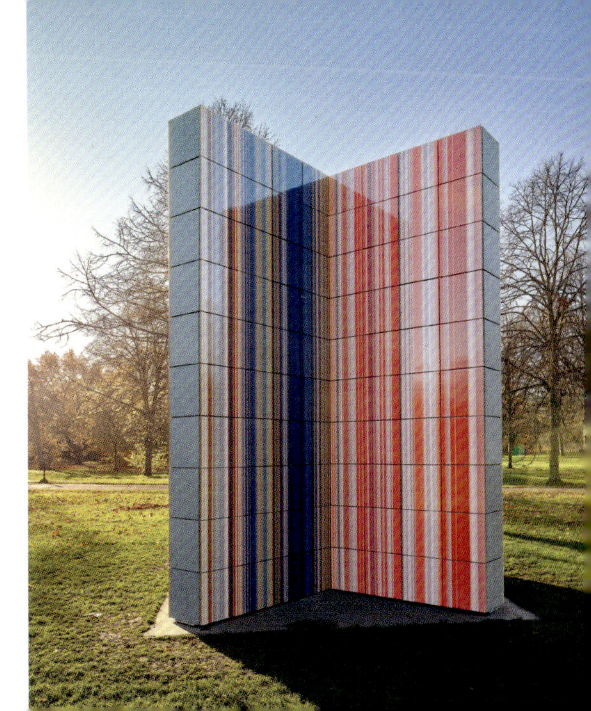

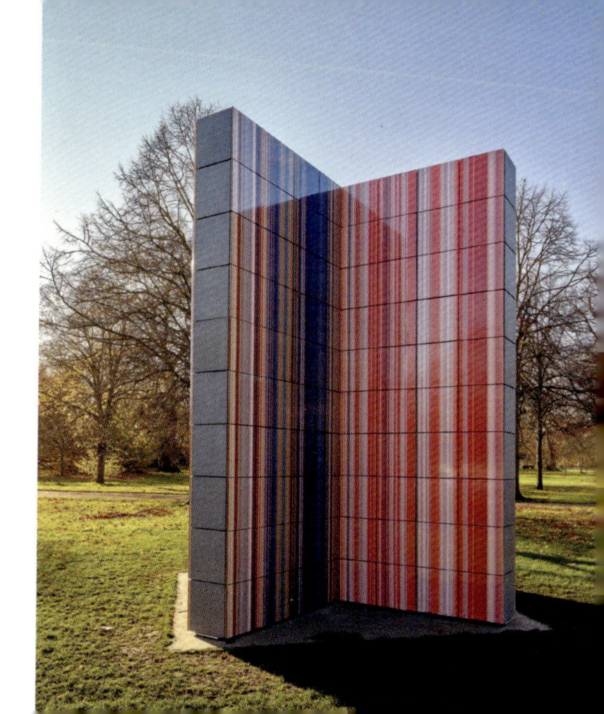

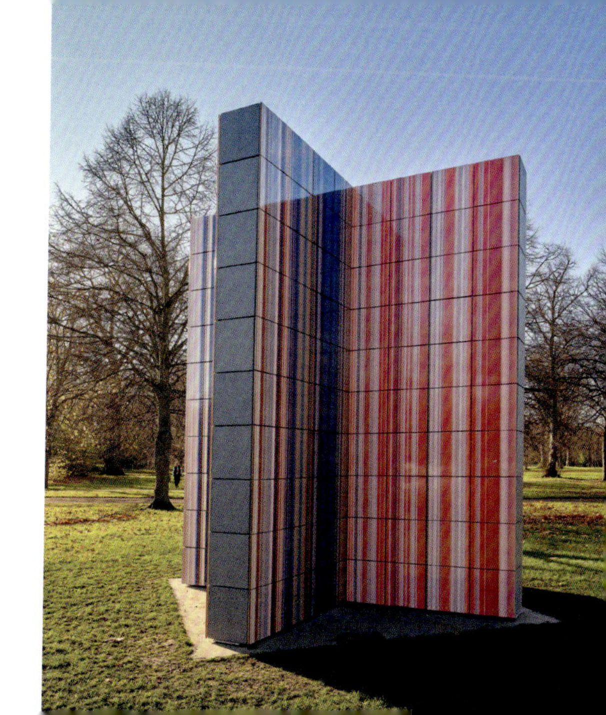

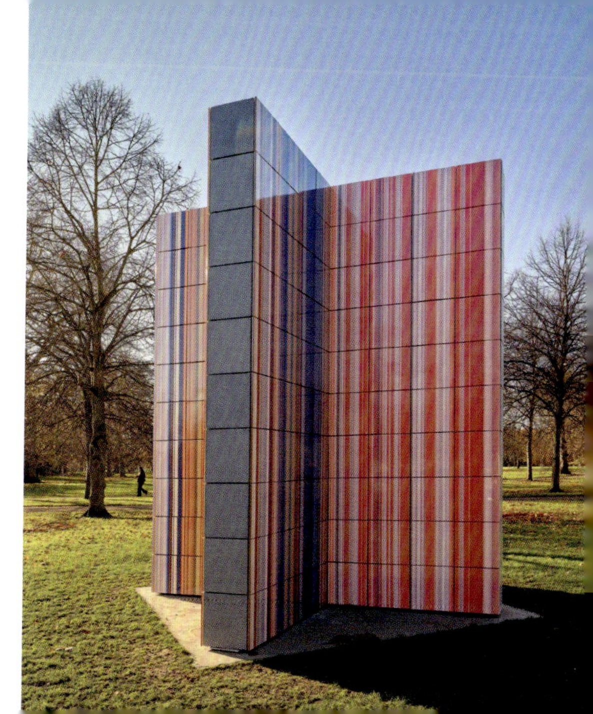

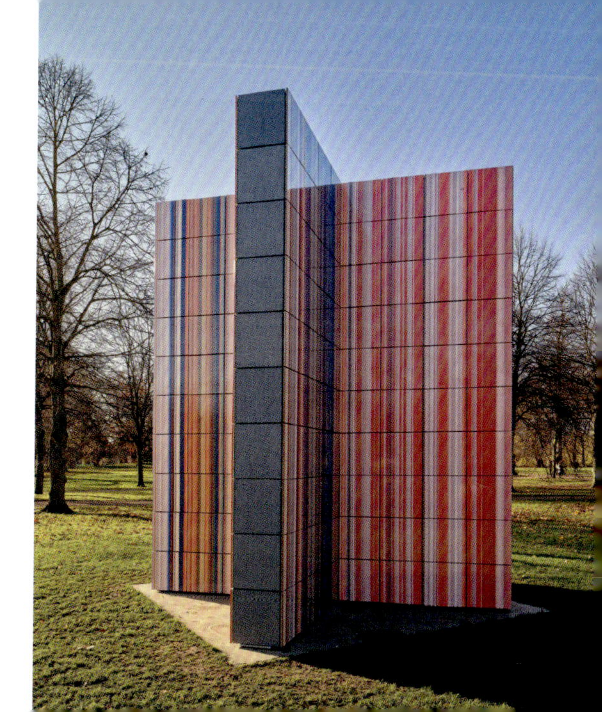

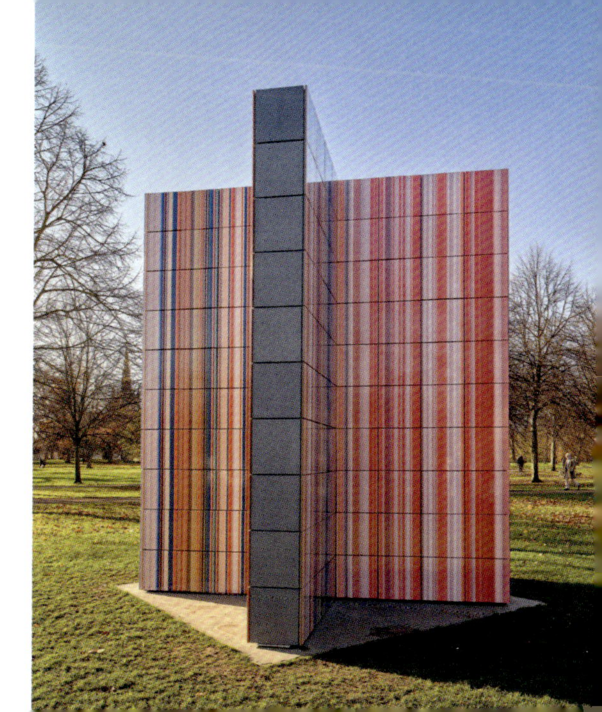

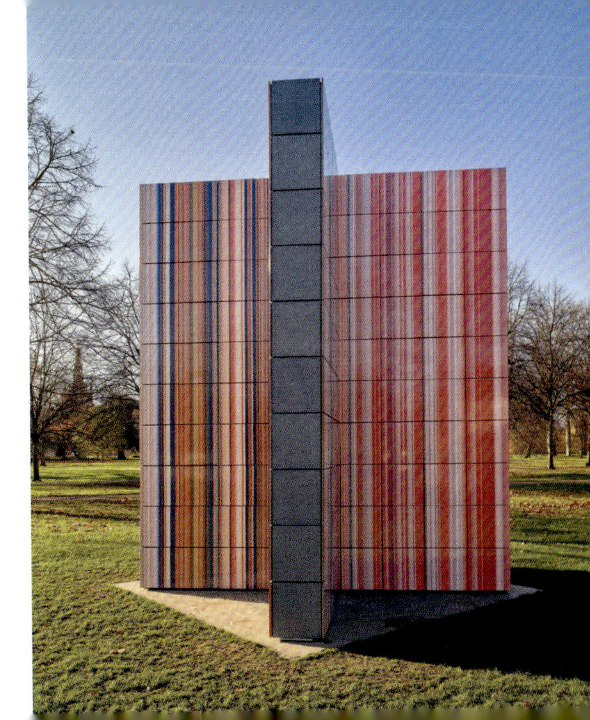

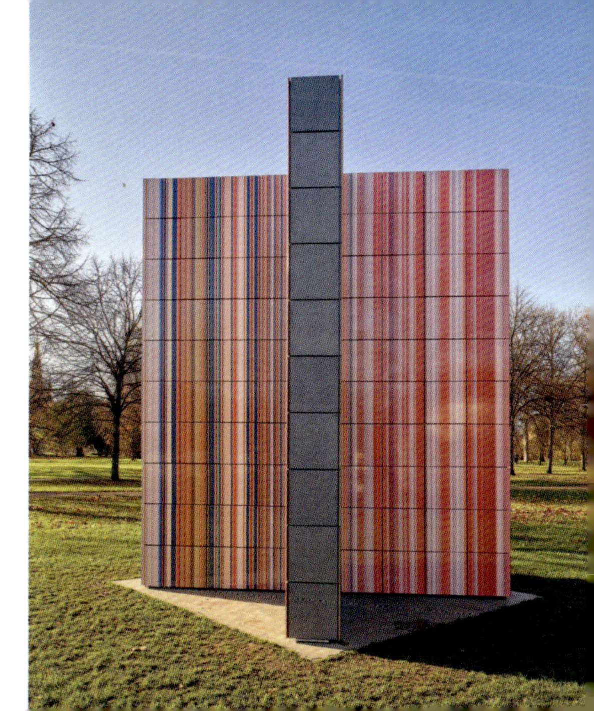

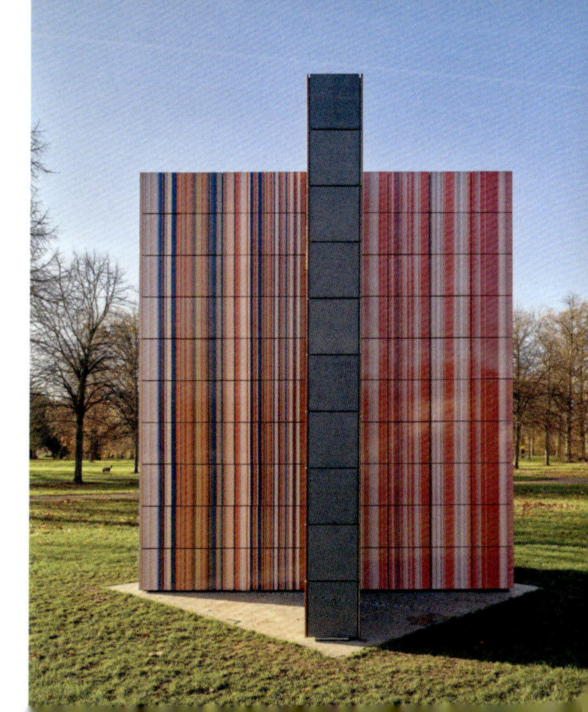

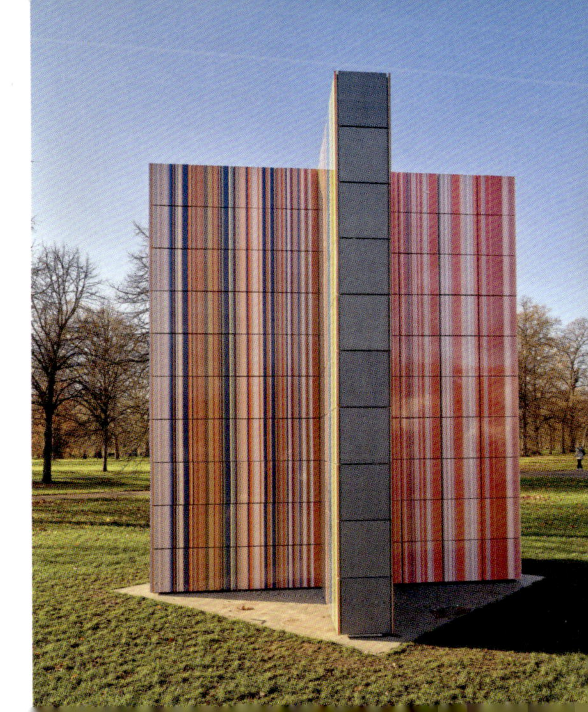

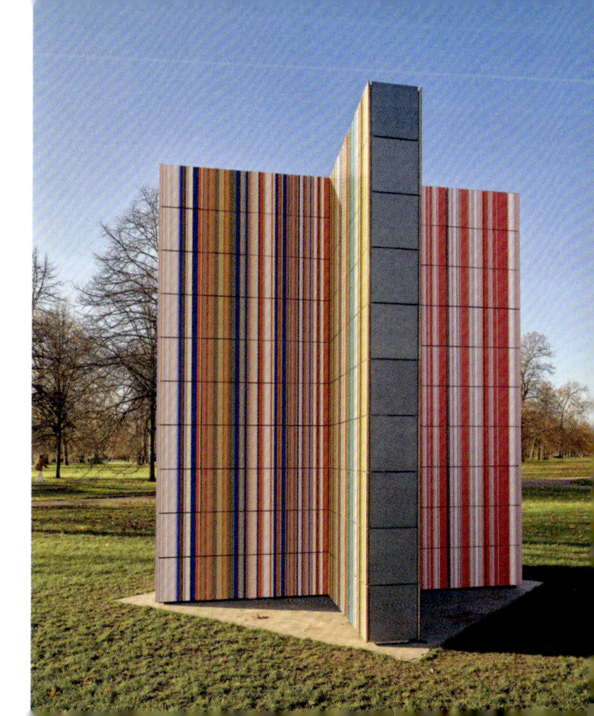

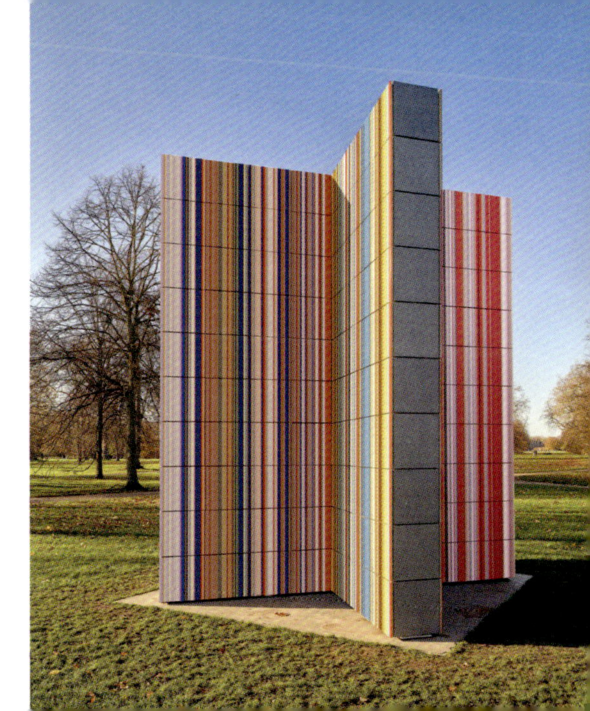

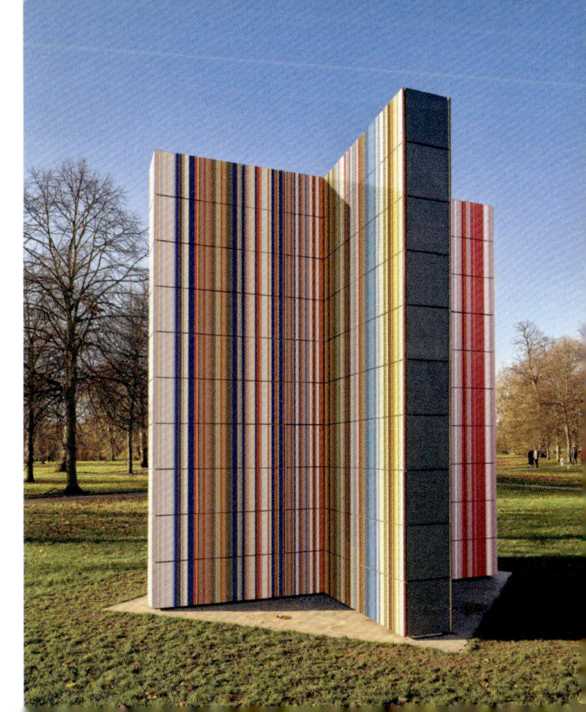

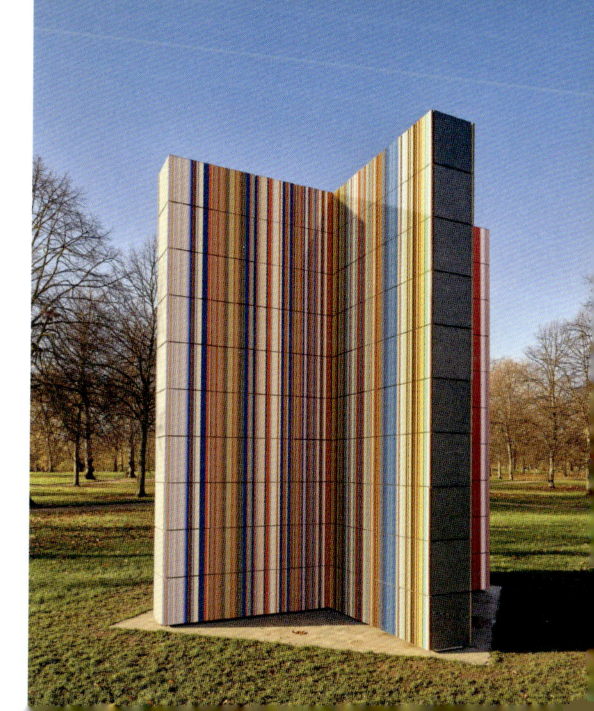

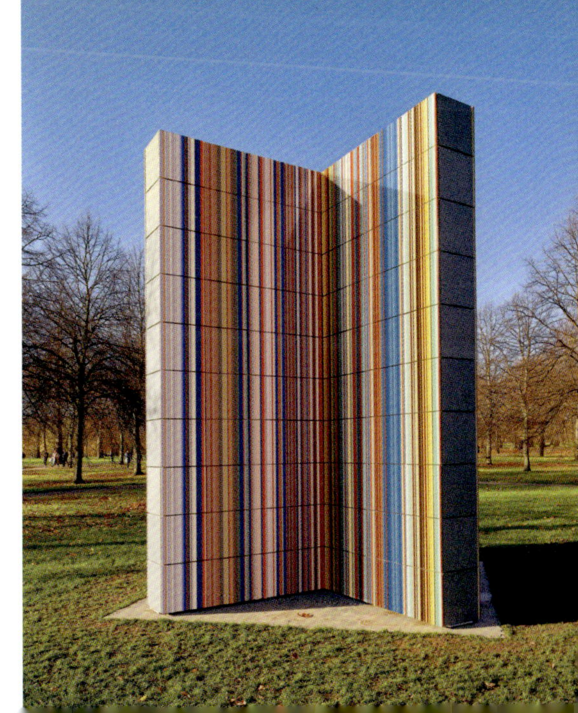

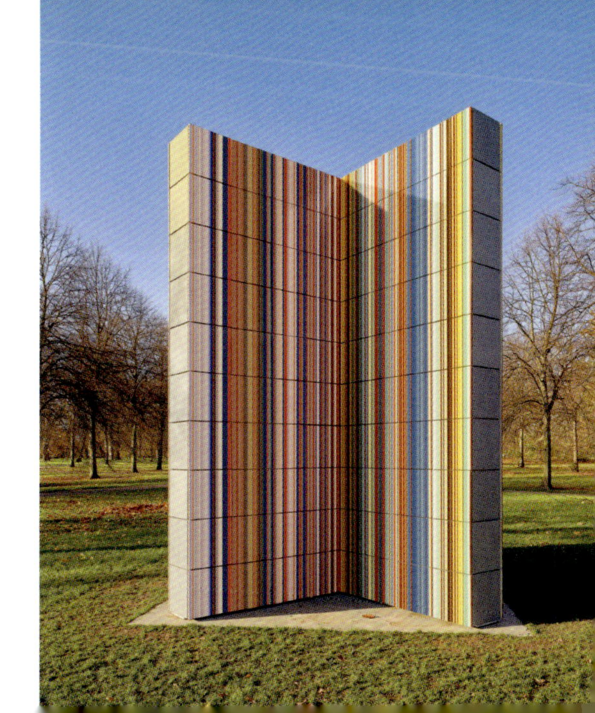

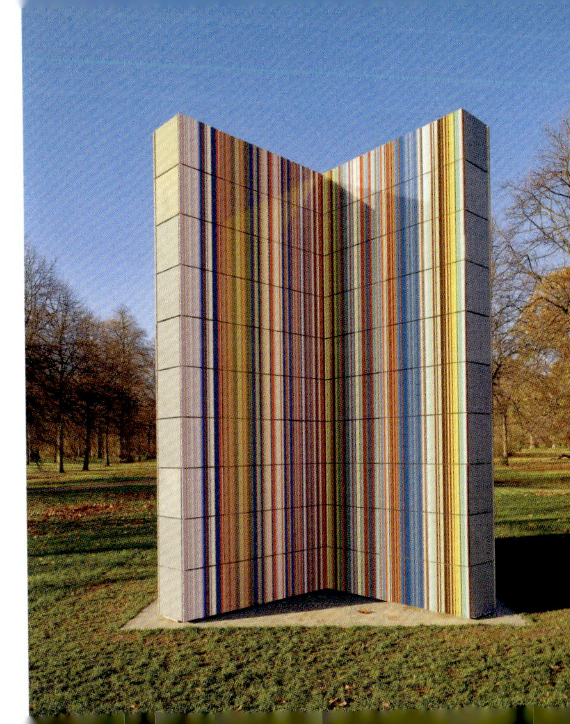

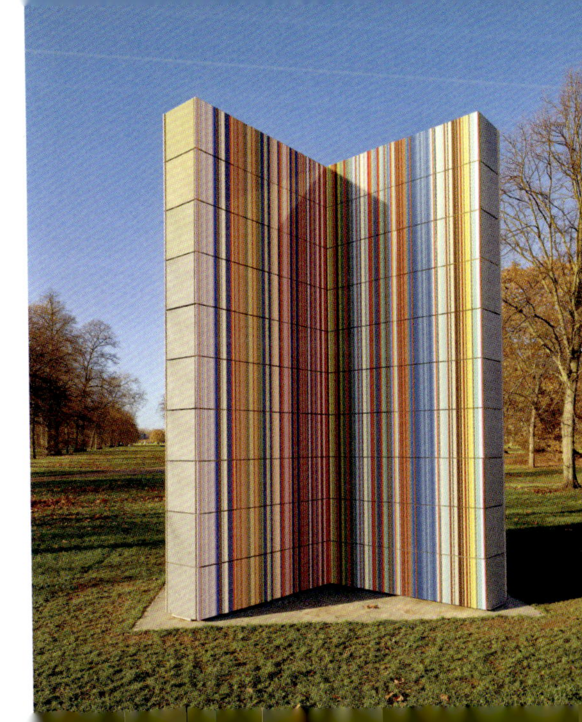

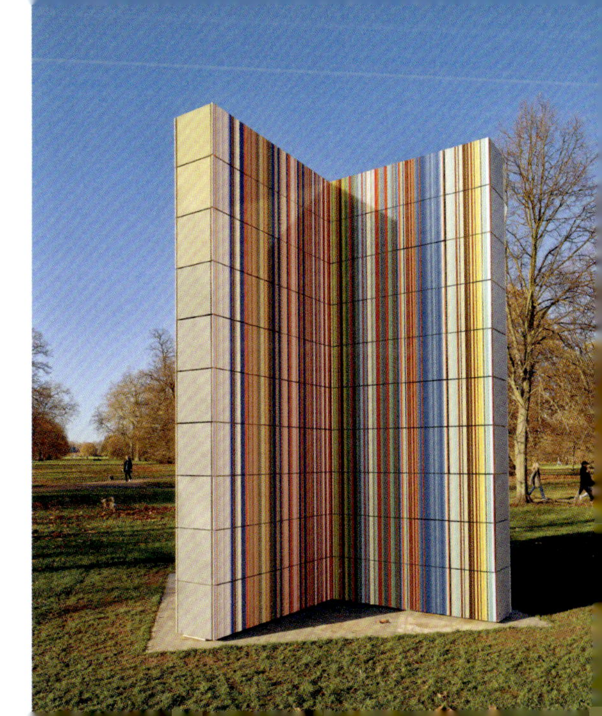

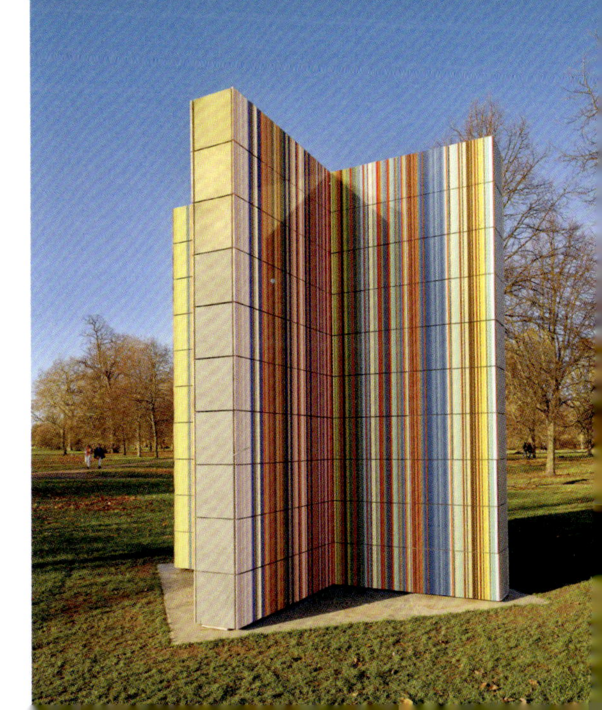

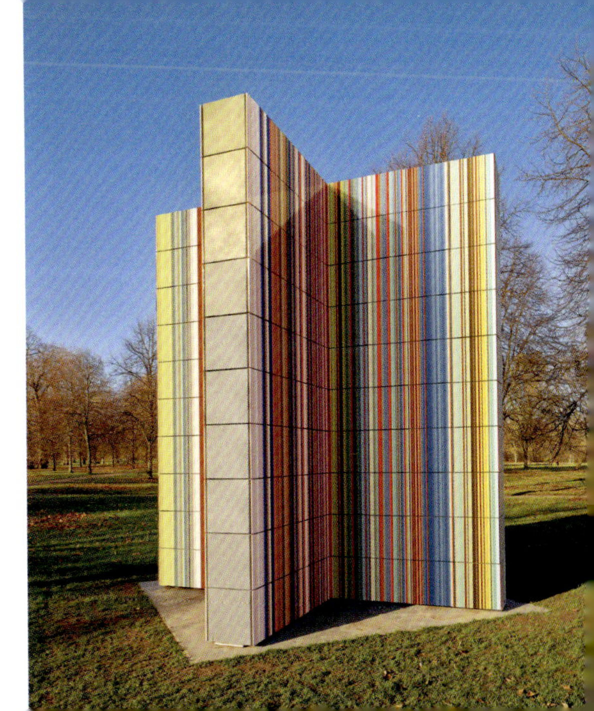

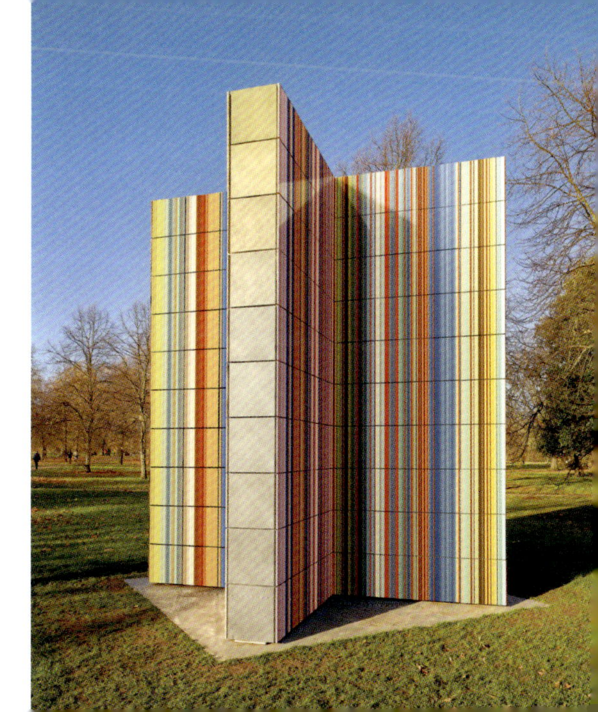

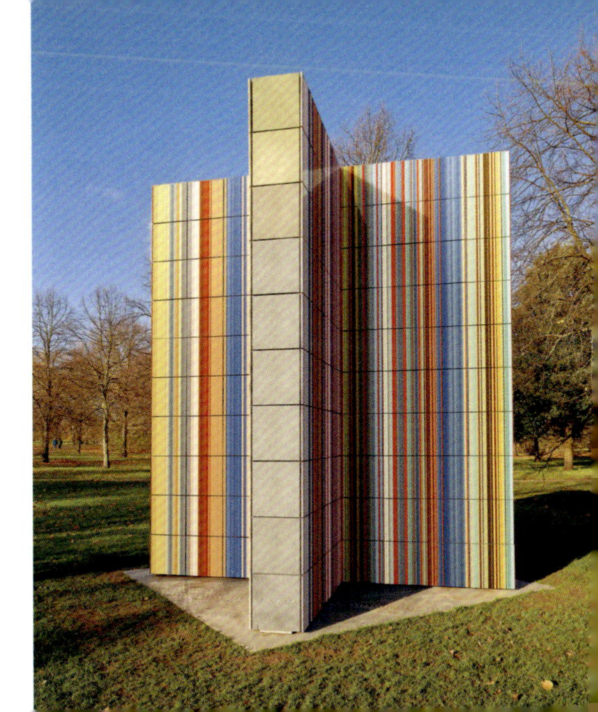

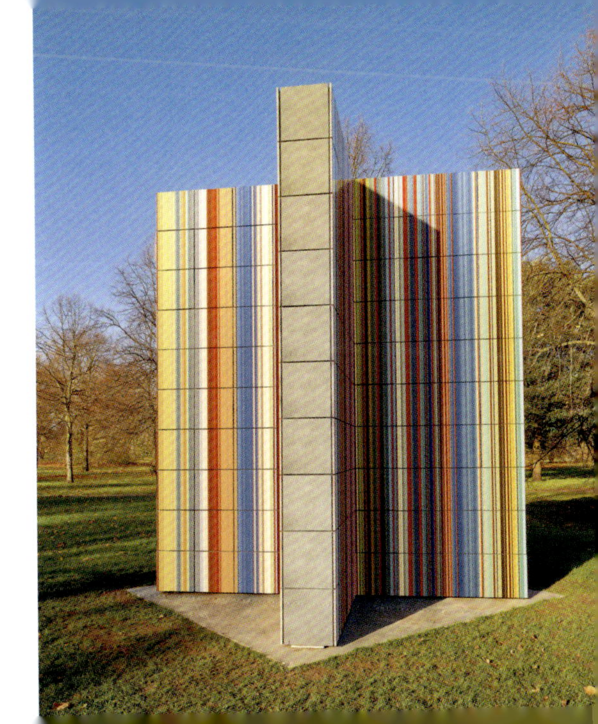

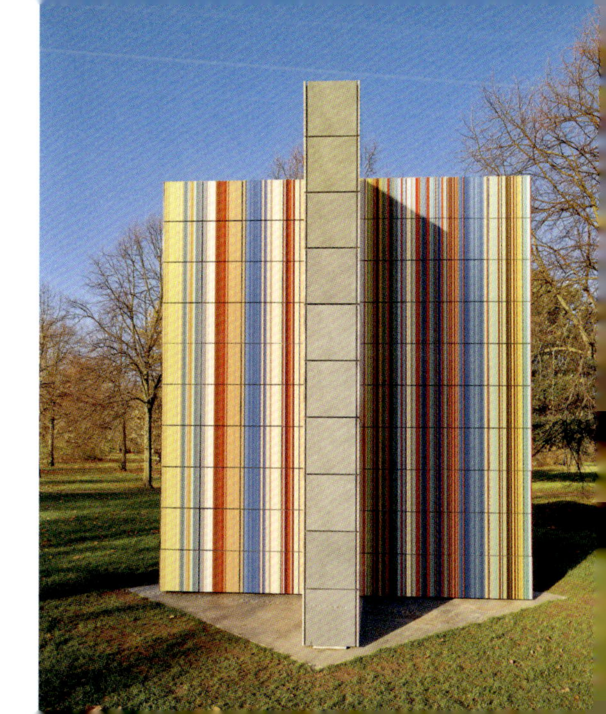

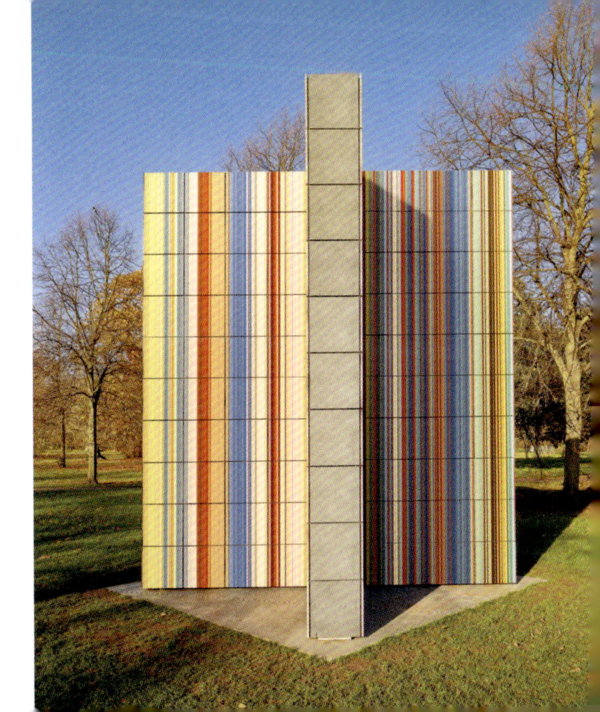

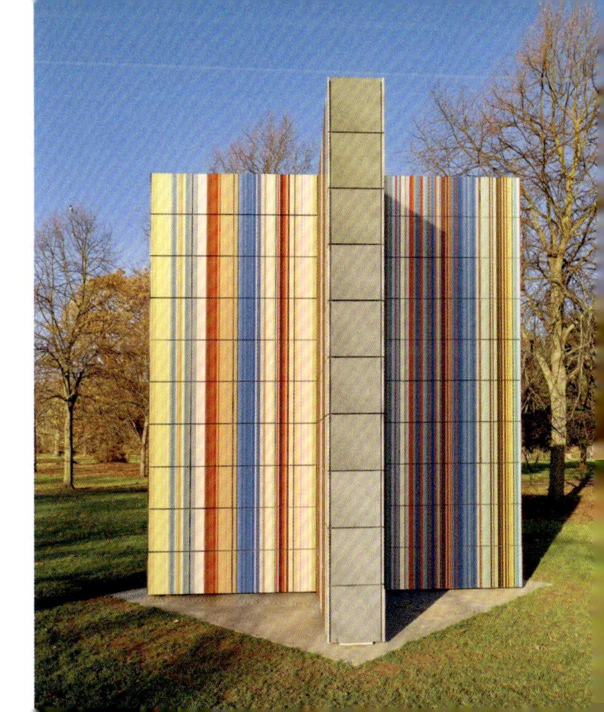

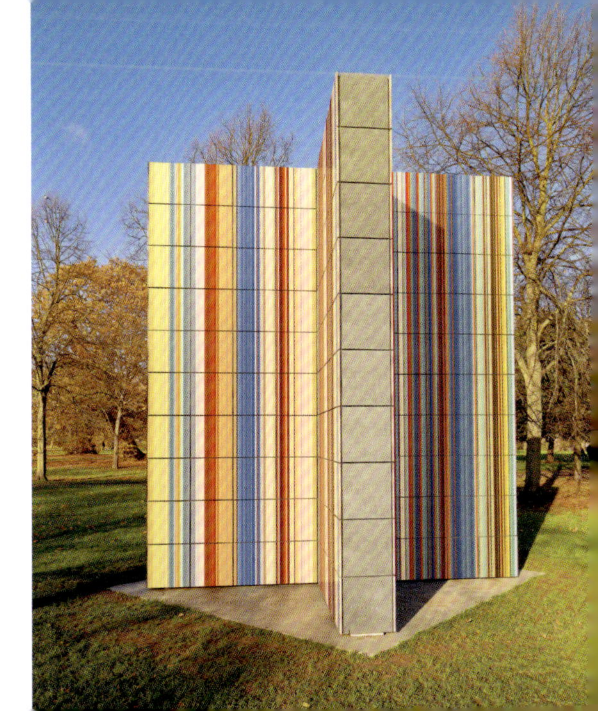

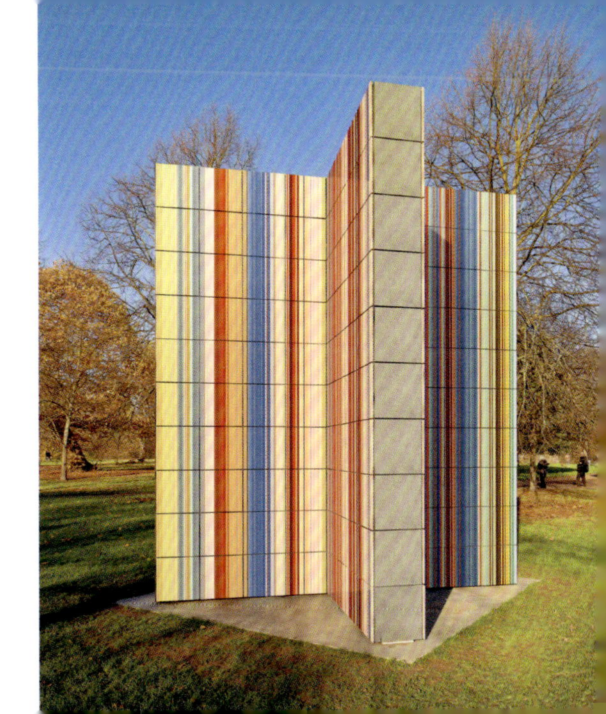

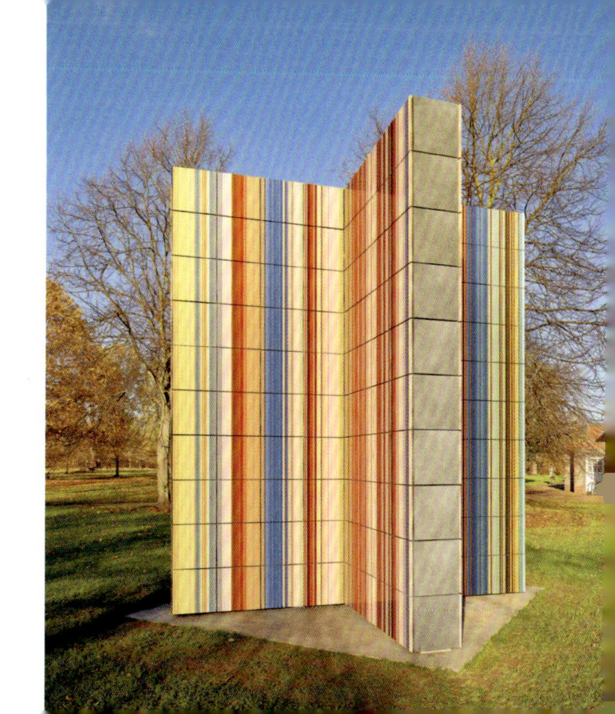

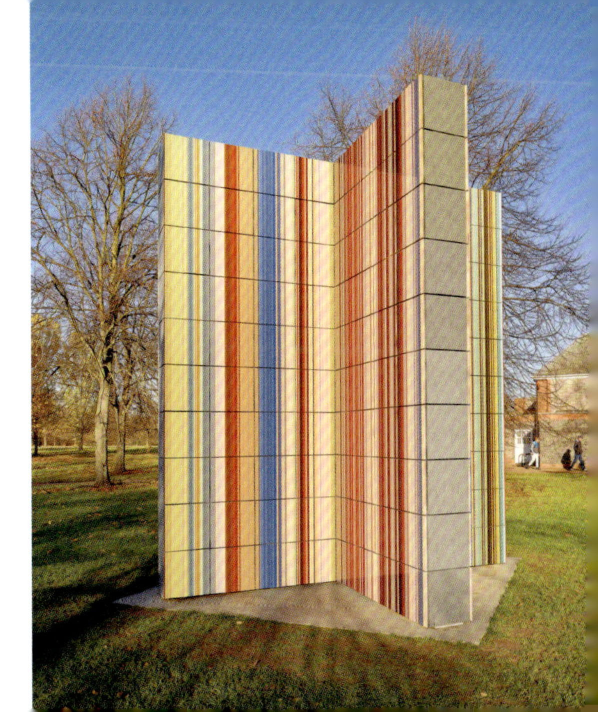

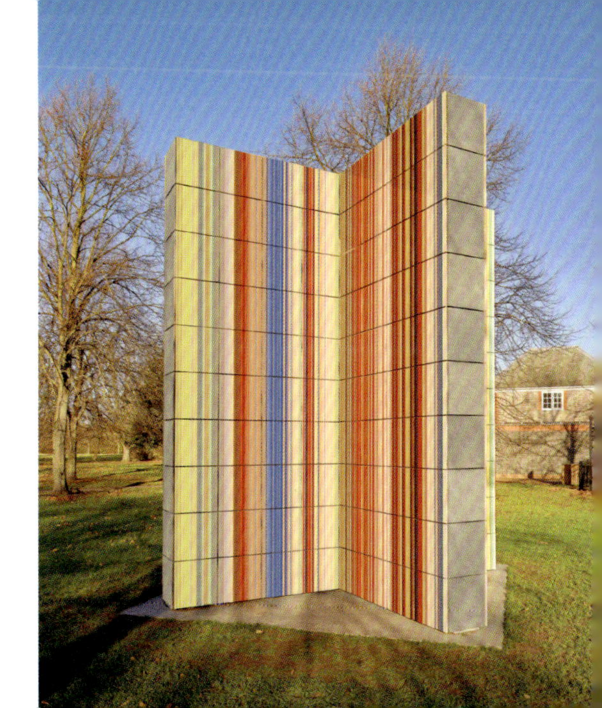

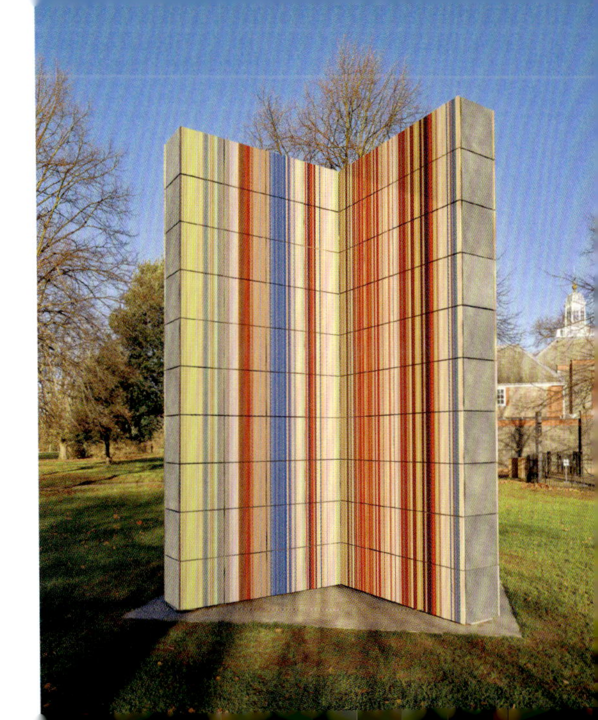

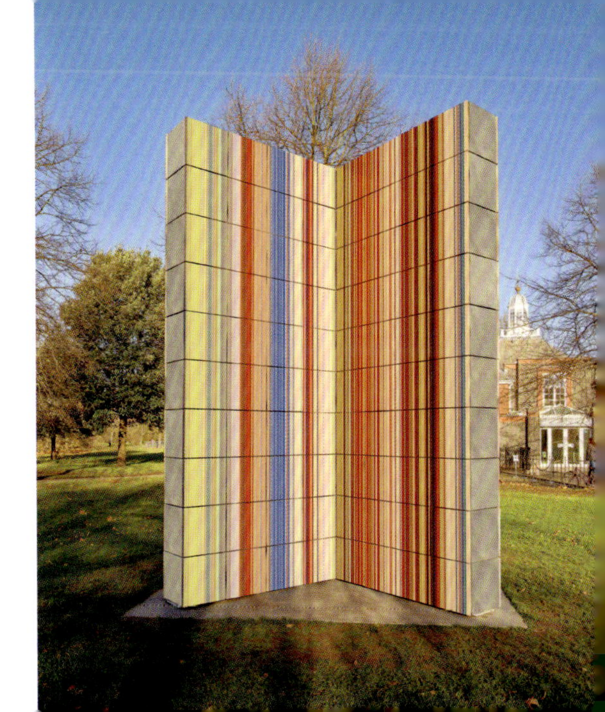

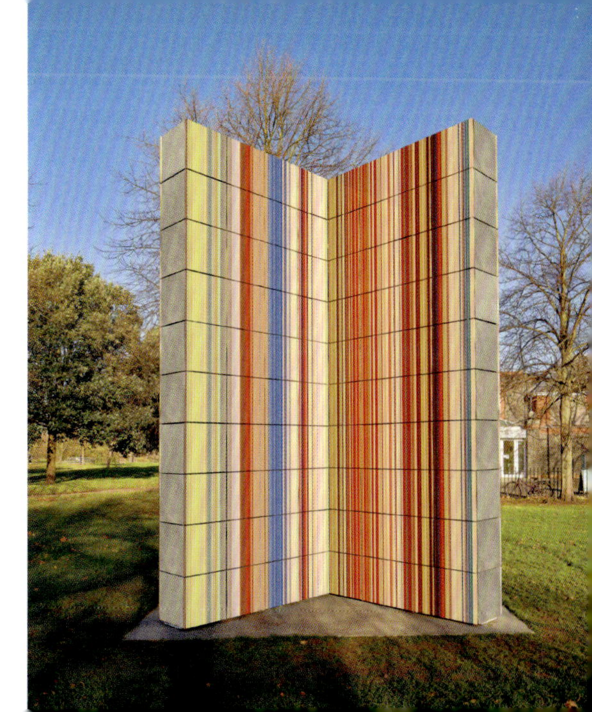

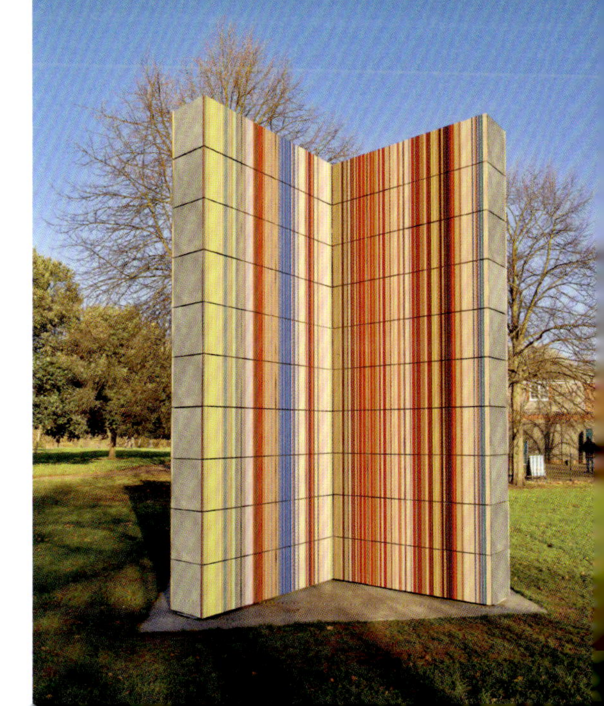

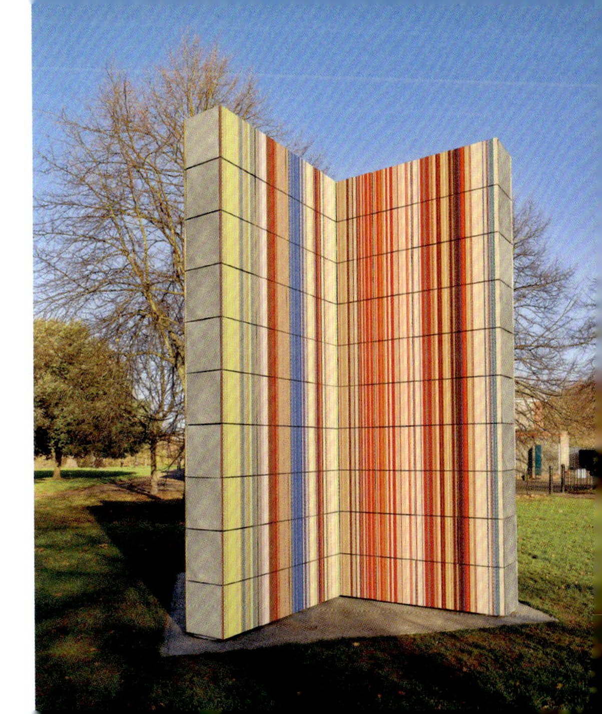

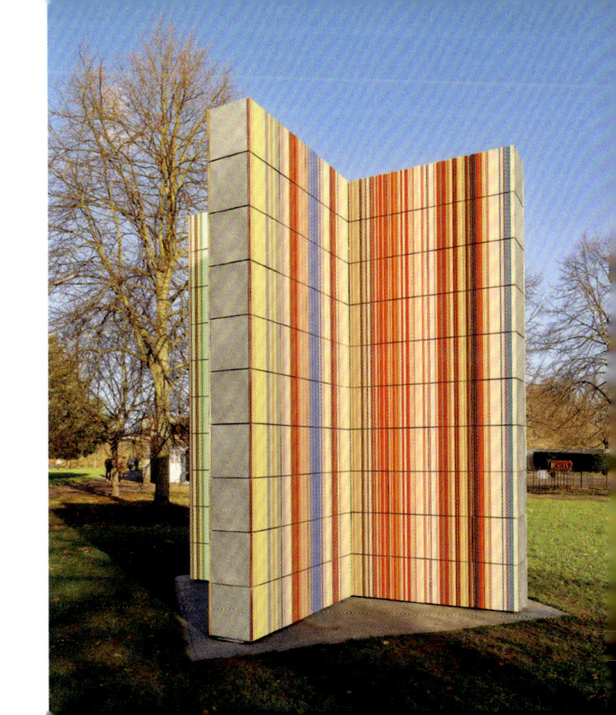

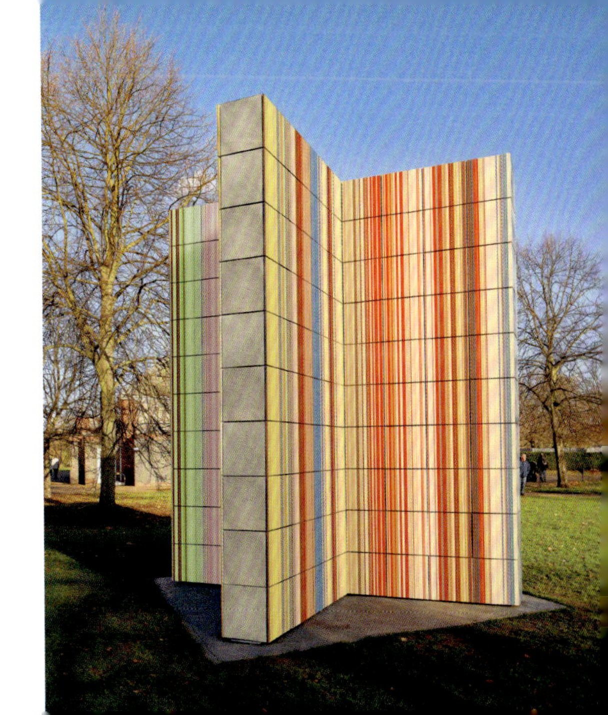

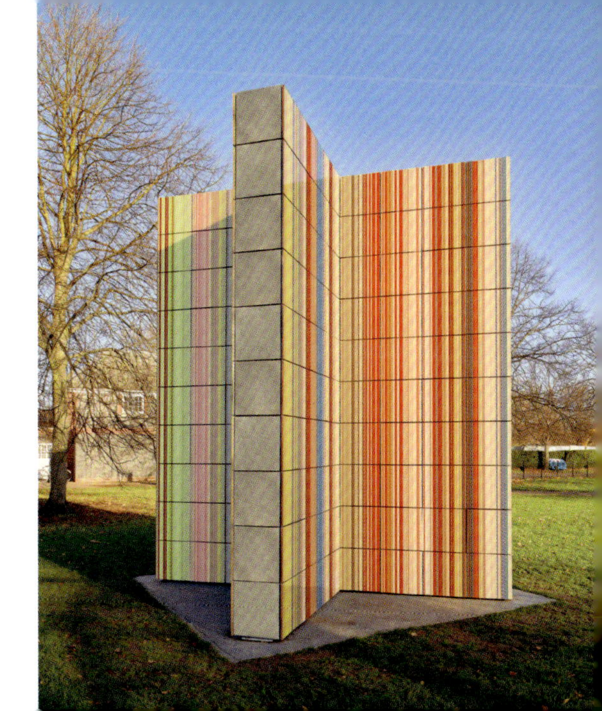

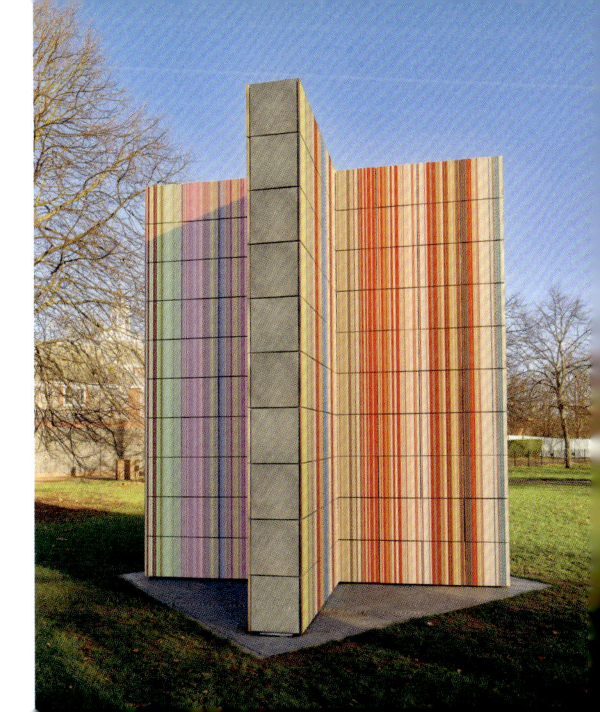

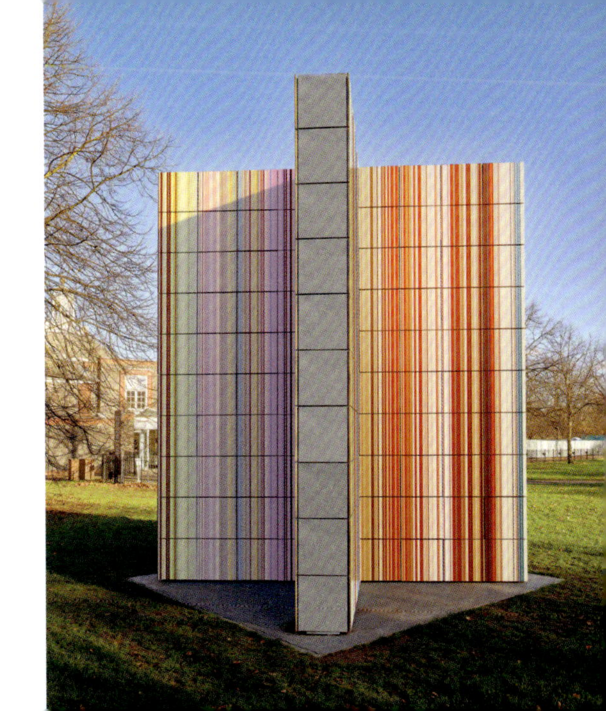

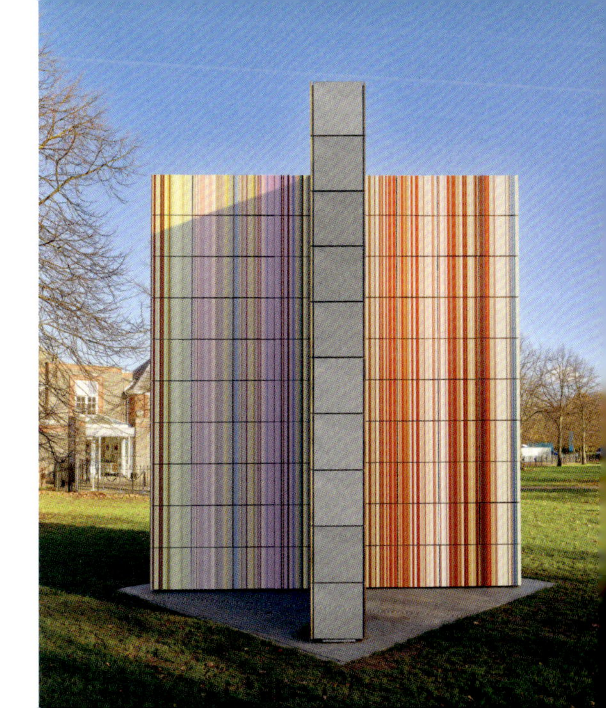

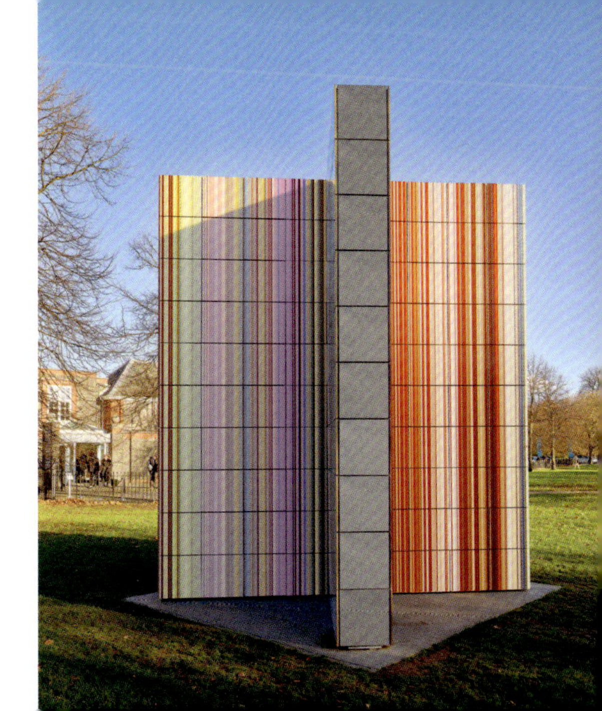

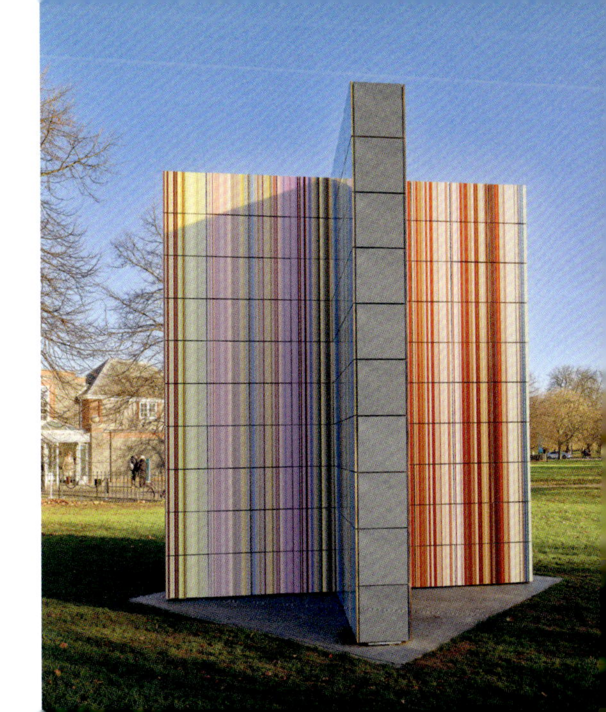

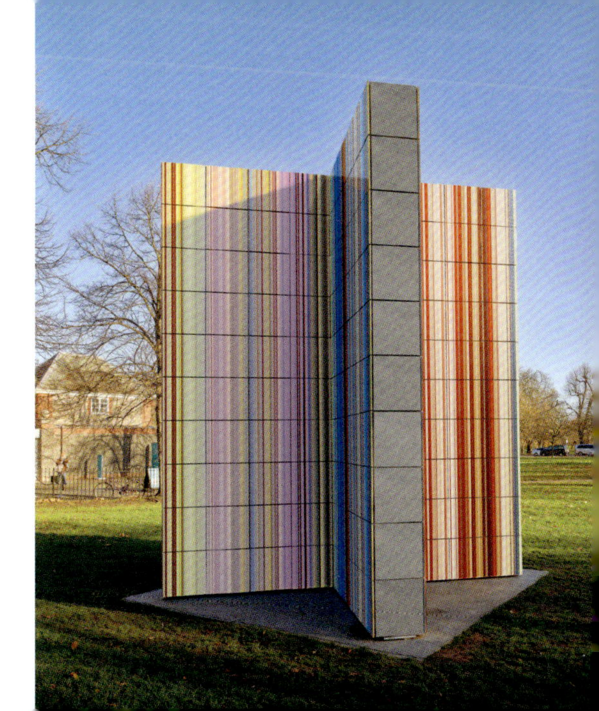

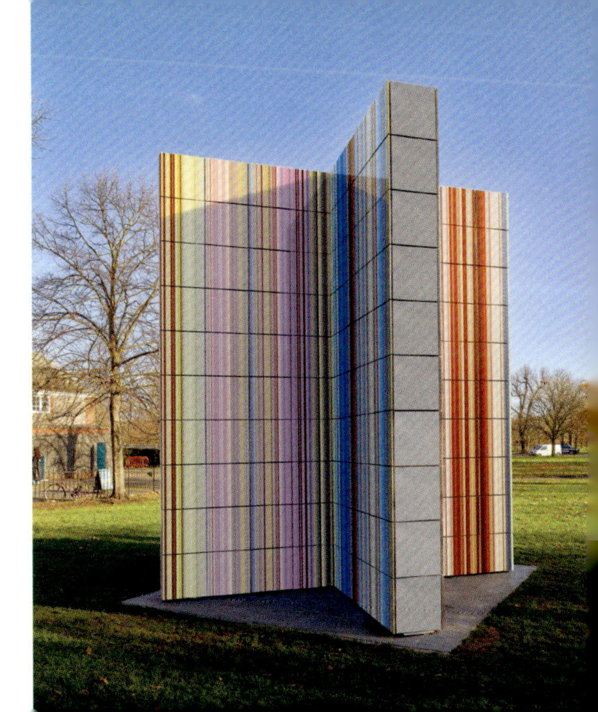

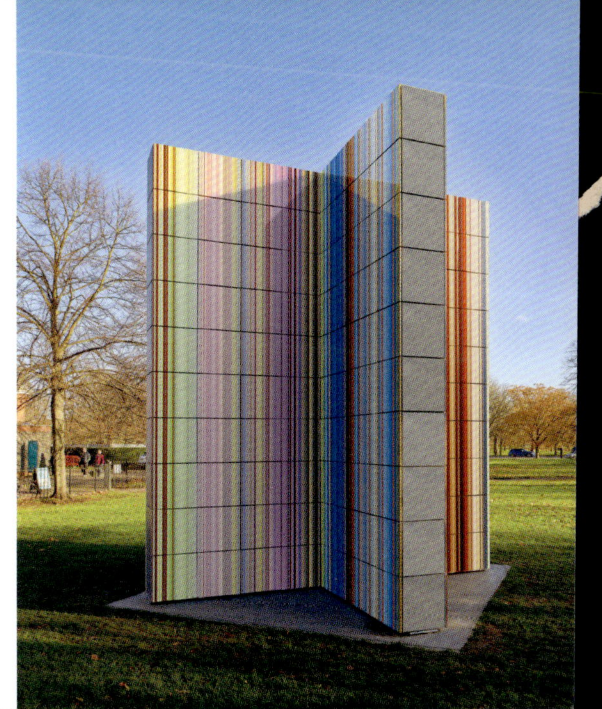

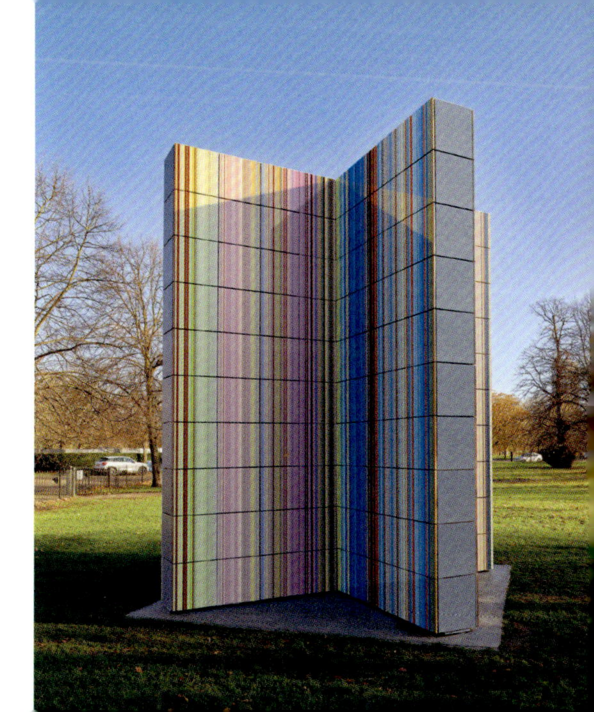

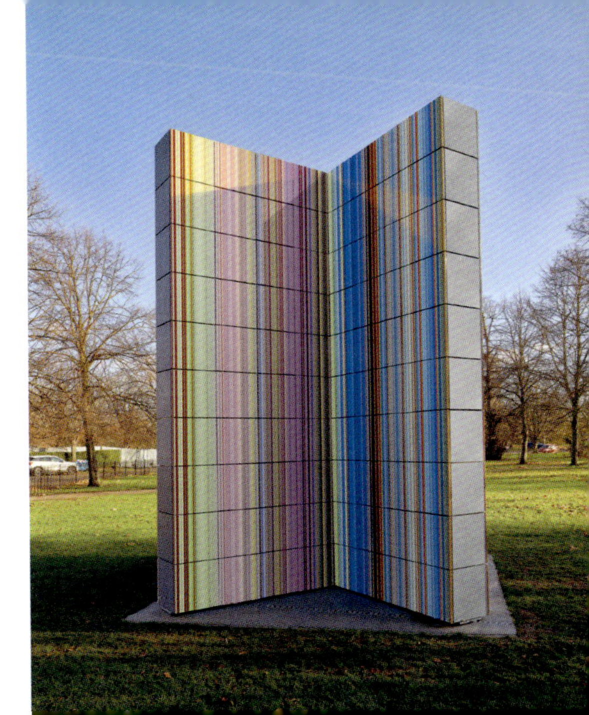

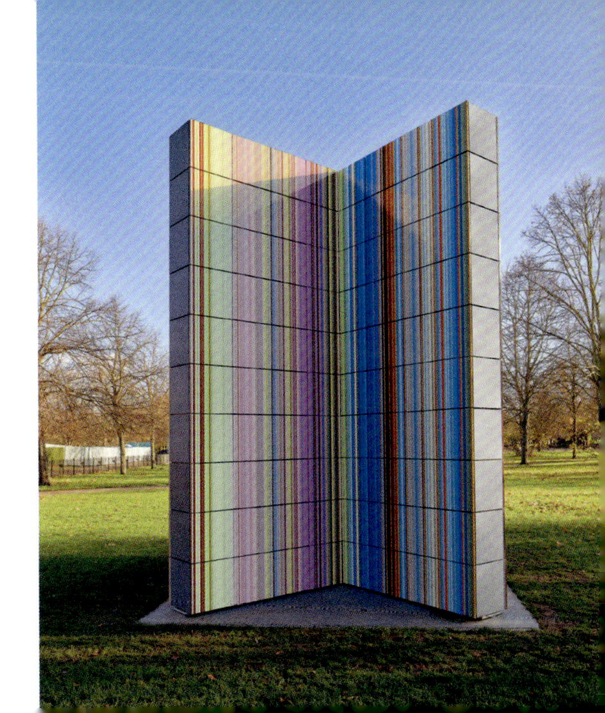

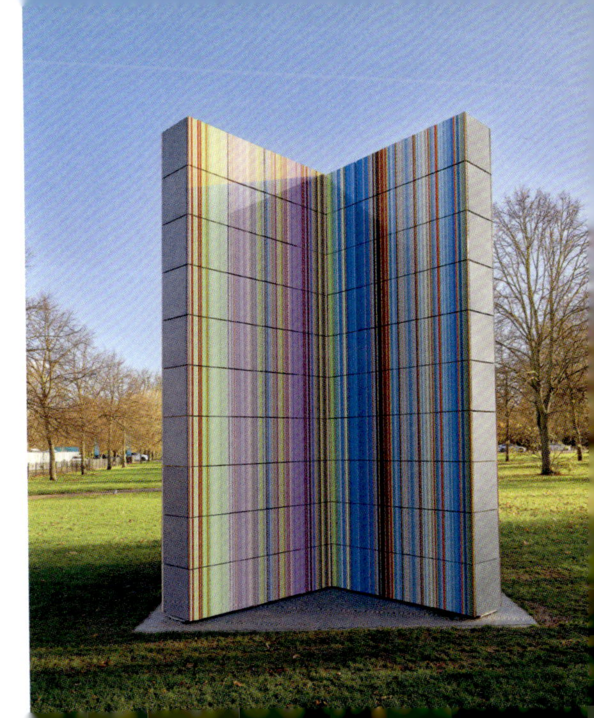

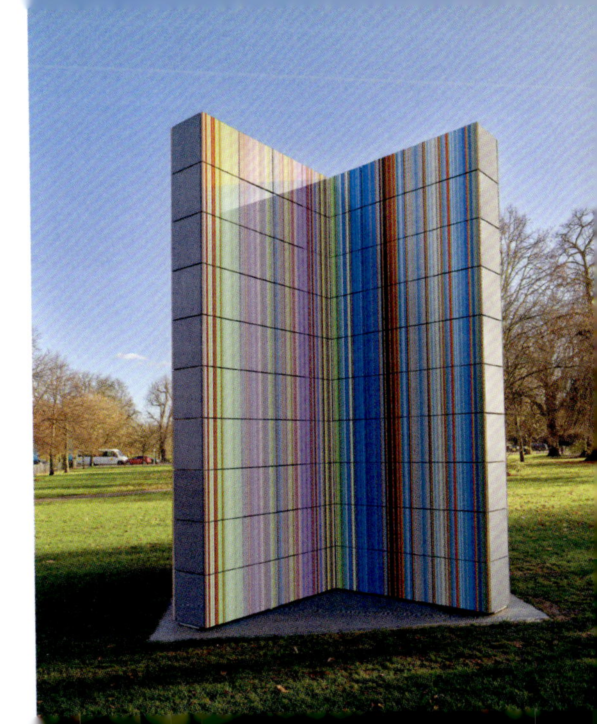

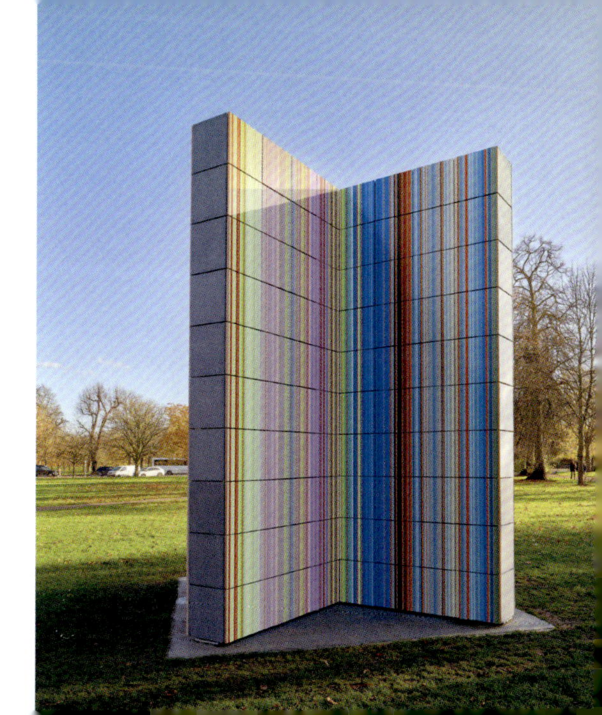

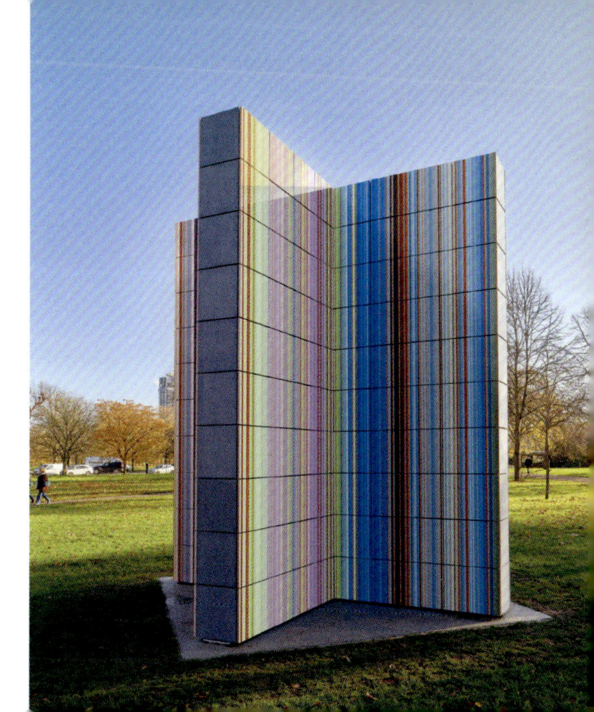

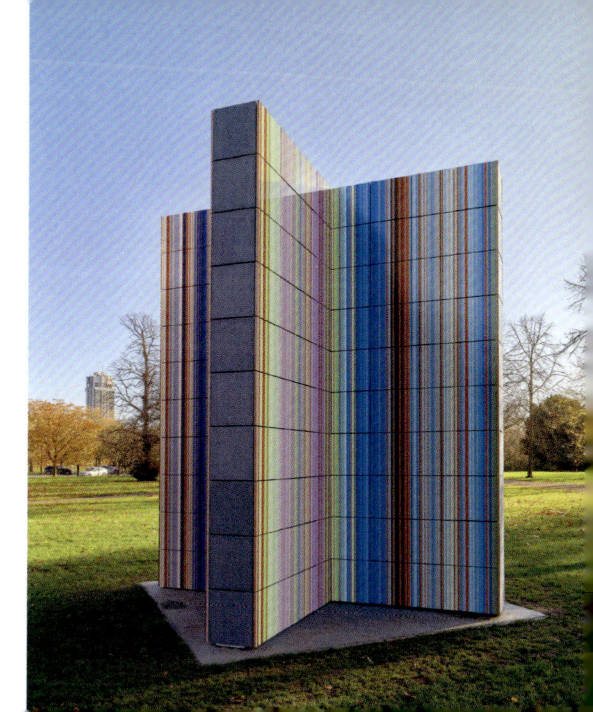

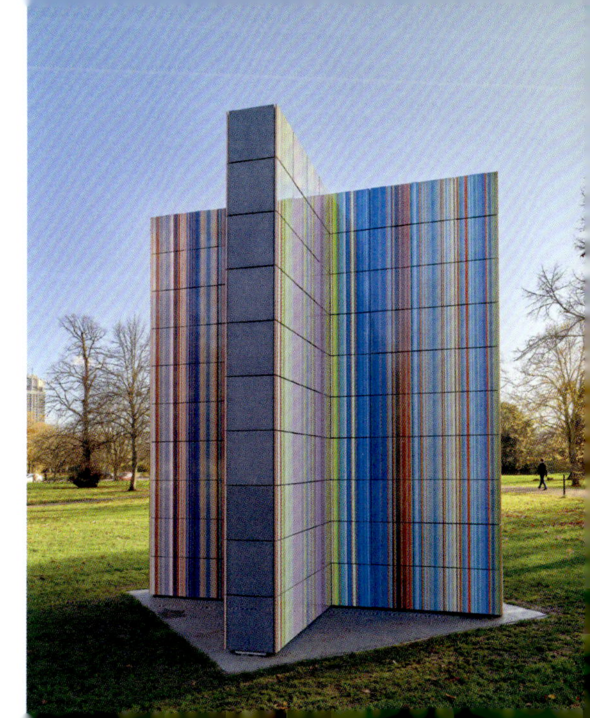

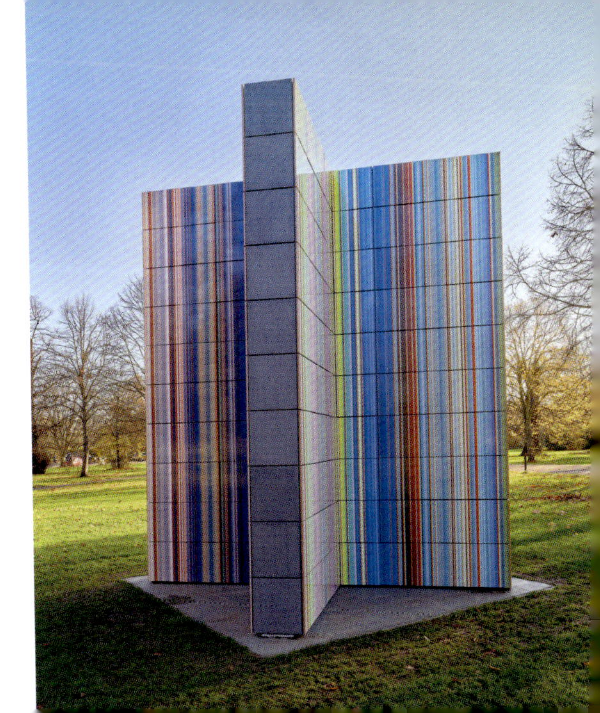

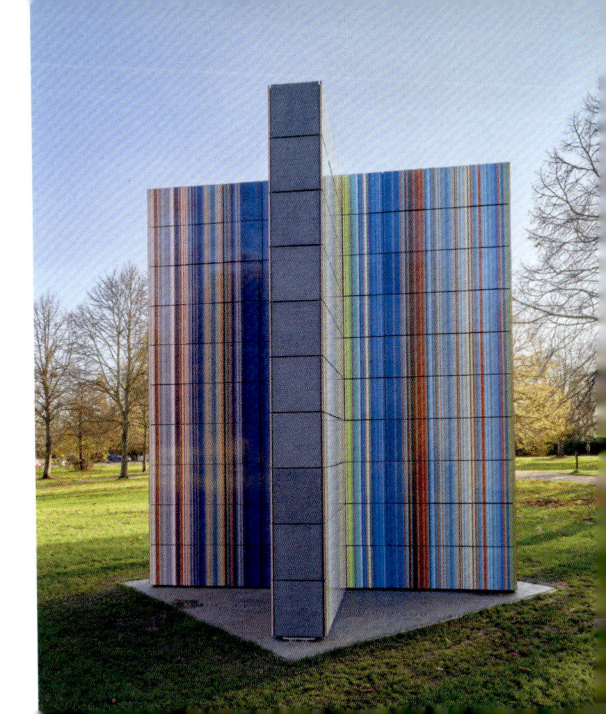

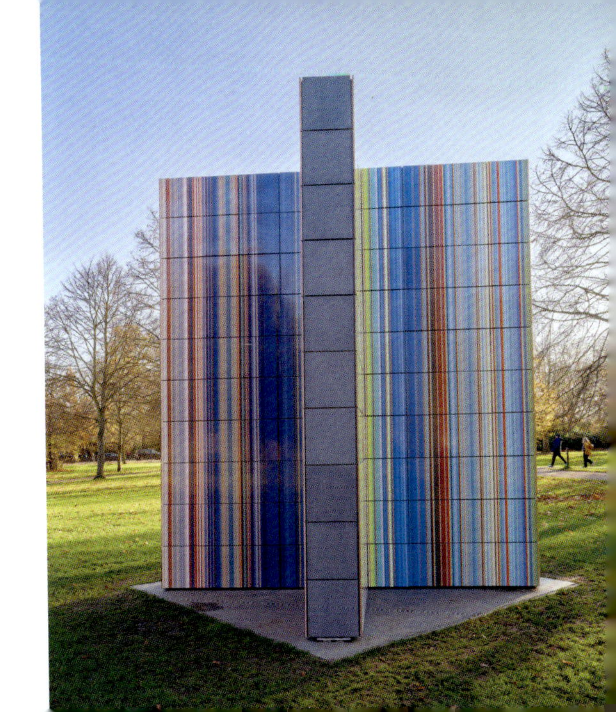

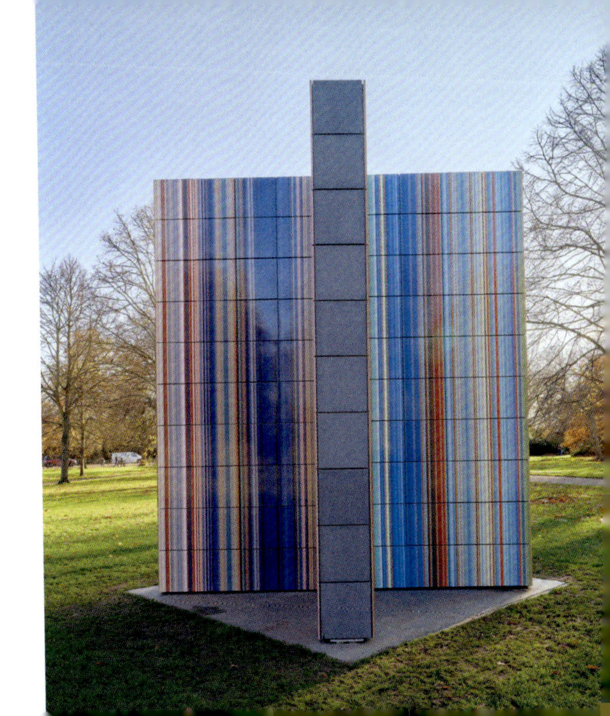

ISBN 978 1 911736 36 3

Photography by Prudence Cuming Associates Ltd
Edited by Rebecca Morrill
Proofread by Kim Scott
Designed by Sylvia Ugga
Production by Sarah McLaughlin
Printed in Belgium by Graphius

Publisher: HENI Publishing, London, United Kingdom
EU Authorised Representative: Easy Access System Europe – Mustamäe tee 50, 10621 Tallinn, Estonia
gpsr.requests@easproject.com

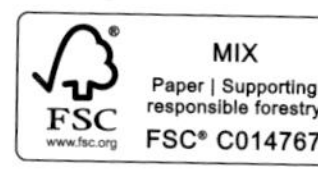